D1390515

The Royal Court The...
presents

THE STRIP

by Phyllis Nagy

First performed at the Royal Court Theatre on 23rd February 1995.

The Royal Court Theatre is financially assisted by the Royal Borough of Kensington and Chelsea.

Recipient of a grant from the Theatre Restoration Fund & from the Foundation for Sport & the Arts.

The Royal Court's Play Development Programme is funded by the Audrey Skirball-Kenis Theatre.

The Royal Court Registered Charity number 231242

THE ENGLISH STAGE COMPANY AT THE ROYAL COURT THEATRE

The English Stage Company was formed to bring serious writing back to the stage. The Court's first Artistic Director, George Devine, wanted to create a vital and popular theatre. He encouraged new writing that explored subjects drawn from contemporary life as well as pursuing European plays and forgotten classics. When John Osborne's **Look Back in Anger** was first produced in 1956, it forced British Theatre into the modern age. But, the Court was much more than a home for 'Angry Young Men' illustrated by a repertoire that stretched from Brecht to Ionesco, by way of J P Sartre, Marguerite Duras, Wedekind and Beckett.

The ambition to discover new work which was challenging, innovative and also of the highest quality became the fulcrum of the Company's course of action. Early Court writers included Arnold Wesker, John Arden, David Storey, Ann Jellicoe, N F Simpson and Edward Bond. They were followed by a generation of writers led by David Hare and Howard Brenton, and in more recent years, celebrated house writers have included Caryl Churchill, Timberlake Wertenbaker, Robert Holman and Jim Cartwright. Many of their plays are now regarded as modern classics.

Arnold Wesker's **The Kitchen**

In line with the policy of nurturing new writing, the Theatre Upstairs has mainly been seen as a place for exploration and experiment, where writers learn and develop their skills prior to the demands of the Main Stage auditorium. Anne Devlin, Andrea Dunbar, Sarah Daniels, Jim Cartwright, Clare McIntyre, Winsome Pinnock, and more recently Martin Crimp have benefited from this process. The Theatre Upstairs proved its value as a focal point for new work with the

production of the Chilean writer Ariel Dorfman's **Death and the Maiden**. More recently talented young writers as diverse as Jonathan Harvey (joint winner of this year's John Whiting Award), Adam Pernak, Phyllis Nagy, Biyi Bandele-Thomas, Gregory Motton and Kevin Elyot, have been shown to great advantage in this space (Elyot's **My Night With Reg** transferred to the Criterion Theatre in November).

1991-1994 were record-breaking years at the box-office with capacity houses for productions of **Top Girls**, **Three Birds Alighting on a Field**, **Faith Healer**, **Death and the Maiden**, **Six Degrees of Separation**, **King Lear**, **Oleanna**, **Hysteria**, **Cavalcaders** and **The Kitchen**.

Death and the Maiden and **Six Degrees of Separation** won the Olivier Award for Best Play in 1992 and 1993 respectively. **Hysteria** won 1994's Olivier Award for Best Comedy, and also the Writer's Guild Award for Best West End Play. **My Night with Reg** won the 1994 Writer's Guild Award for Best Fringe Play, and the Evening Standard Award for Best Comedy. Jonathan Harvey won the 1994 Evening Standard Drama Award for Most Promising Playwright, for **BABIES**.

After nearly four decades, the Royal Court's aims remain consistent with those established by George Devine. The Royal Court Theatre is still a major focus in the country for the production of new work. Scores of plays first seen in Sloane Square are now part of the national and international dramatic repertoire.

John Sessions in Kevin Elyot's **My Night With Reg**

VEGAS....

Las Vegas daylight, like Greek
daylight, makes the polychrome
temples stand out proud and clear in
the desert. This is a quality hard to
catch on film. No photographs of the
Acropolis do it justice. And Las Vegas
is better known for its night light than
its daylight.

Surrounded by the Mojave Desert, Las Vegas is one of the most remote major
American cities. At night it is possible to see the glow from the city's billion
neon bulbs from 50 miles away.

Gambling in the state of Nevada was legalised permanently in 1931. That same
year Nevada's legislature enacted liberal marriage and divorce laws as part of
a scheme to attract tourists. Weddings can be performed without a blood test or
a waiting period. Divorces can be obtained after a six-week residency. In Las
Vegas alone, 80,000 marriages are performed each year with $3 million spent on
marriage licences.

Nevada is America's fastest growing state and Las Vegas (population 850,000)
its fastest growing city, with four per cent annual population growth. It is
second only to Disney World (Florida) as America's most popular tourist
destination. Las Vegas attracts 24 million tourists annually. $25 billion a year is
gambled there; $5 billion a year is lost by gamblers.

Las Vegas is home to 450 religious congregations, nearly a third of which are
Mormon. At the Guardian Angel Cathedral, just east of the Strip, a special
tourist mass is held every Saturday, at which gamblers pray for luck and drop
casino chips into the church's collection plates. Each week a priest cashes in the
chips at Caesar's Palace.

The gambling room is always very dark;
the patio, always very bright. But both
are enclosed: the former has no
windows, and the latter is open only to
the sky. The combination of darkness
and enclosure of the gambling room
and its subspaces makes for privacy,
protection, concentration, and control.
The intricate maze under the low
ceiling never connects with outside
light or outside space. This disorients
the occupant in space and time. One
loses track of where one is and when it
is. Time is limitless, because the light
of noon and midnight are exactly the
same.

Nine out of ten tourists gamble while visiting Las Vegas. The average bankroll of a typical gambler is **$500**. Blackjack, craps, video poker and baccarat are the most advantageous games to bettors, with baccarat providing the house with little more than a one per cent advantage. Roulette, keno and slot machines give the house an advantage of between 5 and 35 per cent.

The Strip....

In 1941 **Thomas Hull**, owner of a chain of California motor inns, built the El Rancho Vegas hotel/casino just outside city limits on Highway 91. One year later, the Last Frontier Hotel was opened a mile down the road. Thus the Strip, a three and a half mile stretch of Las Vegas Boulevard between Hacienda and Sahara Avenues, was born.

> Like the complex architectural accumulations of the Roman Forum, the Strip by day reads as chaos if you perceive only its forms and exclude its symbolic content. The Forum, like the Strip, was a landscape of symbols with layers of meaning evident in the location of roads and buildings, buildings representing earlier buildings, and the sculpture piled all over. Formally the Forum was an awful mess; symbolically it was a rich mix.

30 casinos line the Strip, including: **Excalibur**, a 4,032-room medieval-theme resort; the **Tropicana**, which boast the only swim-up blackjack in town; the **MGM Grand**, housing the largest casino in the world (171,500 square feet with 3,500 slot machines and 165 gaming tables); and **Circus Circus**, a tent-shaped casino with live circus acts performing over the gamblers' heads.

The Sahara Hotel/Casino has the tallest free-standing neon sign in Las Vegas, measuring 222 feet by 18 feet.

The Luxor Hotel, which opened in 1993, is a 2,526-room bronzed-glass pyramid, 350 feet high and 561 feet wide each side of the base. The centre of the hotel is hollow, and through the atrium (29 million cubic feet) runs the Nile River. The 'trilogy of attractions' offers separate rides inside the atrium: a virtual reality motion machine *In Search of the Obelisk* ($5), an interactive movie *Luxor Live* ($4), and *Theatre of Time* with 3D special effects ($4). The casino on the first floor has up to 100 gaming tables. The Luxor has two shows: **Wayne Newton** is currently appearing in the Pharaoh's Theatre, and Nefertiti's Lounge is featuring **American Superstars** with impersonations of Frank Sinatra, The Temptations and Madonna.

The most popular entertainers in Las Vegas (in no particular order) are: **Wayne Newton**, **Tom Jones**, **Ann-Margret**, **Engelbert Humperdinck**, and the illusionists **Siegfried and Roy**.

United States geography..

VIRGINIA (population 6,216,568).
One of the original 13 States of the Union, Virginia gained statehood in 1788. It is bordered to the north by Washington D.C. and Maryland, to the west by West Virginia and Kentucky, to the south by Tennessee and North Carolina, and to the east by parts of Maryland, the Chesapeake Bay and the Atlantic Ocean. The first and last important battles of the American Civil War were fought in Virginia. It is the birthplace of eight US presidents, and the CIA is headquartered there. Oliver North recently ran on the Republican ticket for the US Senate representing Virginia. He lost, but garnered more votes than expected.

ARLINGTON, VIRGINIA (population 173,800).
An affluent suburb of Washington, D.C., home to many Government employees. What was later to become Arlington National Cemetery was established near the end of the Civil War as a burial ground for Union casualties. The cemetery was set up on the grounds of the Confederate General Robert E. Lee's estate so that when Lee returned to his home, he could see what devastation the Confederacy had wrought on the Union.

ROANOKE, VIRGINIA (population 95,900).
Small city situated in the foothills of the Blue Ridge Mountains, 226 miles southwest of Washington, D.C.

LYNCHBURG, VIRGINIA (population 65,300).
Small city noted for its colleges, 52 miles northeast of Roanoke.

JERICHO, LONG ISLAND.
Suburb of New York City, situated approximately 30 miles east of Manhattan.

SECAUCUS, NEW JERSEY (population 13,719).
Industrial city just five miles from Manhattan, across the Hudson River through the Lincoln Tunnel.

HOBOKEN, NEW JERSEY (population 42,460).
Increasingly trendy city inhabited by professional families, artists and students, three miles from Manhattan, across the Hudson River through the Holland Tunnel.

(*Note: Ava Coo and Calvin Higgins drive more than 2,500 miles across America to get from Jericho to Las Vegas in two weeks. Their route is not the most direct, but it is one of the more interesting.*)

Quotations from *Learning from Las Vegas* by Robert Venturi. Reprinted by permission of the MIT Press, copyright © 1977 The Massachusetts Institute of Technology.

Next at the Court...

Thi s Season is being presented in association with The Royal National Theatre Studio, with sponsorship from The Jerwood Foundation and The Audrey Skirball-KenisTheatre.

MAIN HOUSE
From 6th April
SIMPATICO
by Sam Sheppard

THEATRE UPSTAIRS
From 16th February
THE KNOCKY
by Michael Wynne

From 9th March
UGANDA
by Judith Johnson

From 30th March
THE STEWARD OF CHRISTENDOM
by Sebastian Barry

From 27th April
STAR GAZEY PIE
by James Stock

In The West End

MY NIGHT WITH REG
by Kevin Elyot
at the Criterion Theatre

Box Office 0171-839-4488

THE STRIP

by Phyllis Nagy

CAST *in alphabetical order*

Tina	**Amanda Boxer**
Loretta	**Cheryl Campbell**
Kate Buck	**Nancy Crane**
Lester	**Nicholas Farrell**
Suzy	**Caroline Harker**
Ava Coo	**Deirdre Harrison**
Otto Mink	**Nicholas le Prevost**
Martin	**Patrick O'Kane**
Calvin	**William Osborne**
Tom Warner	**John Padden**

Director	**Steven Pimlott**
Designer	**Tobias Hoheisel**
Design assistant	**Patrick Watkinson**
Lighting Designer	**Peter Mumford**
Sound	**Paul Arditti**
Stage Manager	**Maris Sharp**
Deputy Stage Manager	**Helen Bond**
Assistant Stage Manager	**Rupert Carlile**
Production Photographer	**Ivan Kyncl**
Leaflet Design	**The Loft**

BIOGRAPHIES

PHYLLIS NAGY (writer)

Phyllis was born in New York City and now lives in London.

For the Royal Court: Weldon Rising (in association with Liverpool Playhouse).

Other recent plays include: Disappeared (Leicester Haymarket/Midnight Theatre Company; second prize, Mobil International Playwriting Competition, 1992); Butterfly Kiss (Almeida Theatre); Trip's Cinch (Actors Theatre of Louisville); The Scarlet Letter (Classic Stage Company, Denver Centre Theatre Company). Radio: The Strip (Radio 4).

Awards and Fellowships: Arts Council Playwright-in-Residence, Royal Court Theatre; National Endowment for the Arts playwriting fellowships; New York Foundation for the Arts playwriting fellowship; McKnight Foundation playwriting fellowship.

Phyllis is currently under commission to Hampstead Theatre and the Royal Court Theatre.

PAUL ARDITTI (sound designer)

For the Royal Court: Blasted, Peaches, The Editing Process, Babies, Some Voices, Thyestes, My Night With Reg, The Kitchen, The Madness of Esme and Shaz, Hammett's Apprentice, Hysteria, Live Like Pigs, Search and Destroy.

Other theatre sound design includes: The Threepenny Opera (Donmar Warehouse); Hamlet (Gielgud); Piaf (Piccadilly); St. Joan (Strand); The Winter's Tale, Cymbeline, The Tempest, Antony & Cleopatra, The Trackers of Oxyrhynchus (Royal National Theatre); The Gift of the Gorgon (RSC & Wyndham's); Orpheus Descending (Theatre Royal, Haymarket & Broadway); The Merchant of Venice (Phoenix & Broadway); A Streetcar Named Desire (Bristol Old Vic); The Winter's Tale (Manchester Royal Exchange); The Wild Duck (Phoenix); Henry IV, The Ride Down Mount Morgan (Wyndham's); Born Again (Chichester); Three Sisters, Matador (Queen's); Twelfth Night, The Rose Tattoo (Playhouse); Two Gentlemen of Verona, Becket, Cyrano de Bergerac (Theatre Royal, Haymarket); Travesties (Savoy); Four Baboons Adoring the Sun (Lincoln Center, 1992 Drama Desk Award).

Opera includes: Gawain (ROH).

TV includes: The Camomile Lawn.

AMANDA BOXER

London theatre includes: All My Sons, The Merchant of Venice, Othello, The Way of the World, The Importance of Being Earnest (Young Vic); A Touch of the Poet (Young Vic & Comedy Theatre); Strange Snow (Theatro Technis/Best Actress 1991/92 Carling London Fringe Award); Conversations with George Sandburg (Croydon Warehouse); Propaganda Fide, The Red Circle (Old Red Lion); The House of Bernarda Alba (Globe Theatre); A State of Affairs (Duchess Theatre); The Misanthrope (Royal Exchange & Roundhouse); Vassa (Greenwich); Two (Offstage Downstairs); Better in my Dreams (Watermans Art Centre).

New York: The Pixie Led (Judith Anderson Theatre).

Regional theatre includes: Julius Caesar, Absurd Person Singular, Much Ado About Nothing (Manchester Royal Exchange); Death and the Maiden, The Secret Rapture (Manchester Library); Queen Christina (Bristol Old Vic); All's Well That Ends Well, The Rivals (Theatr Clwyd); My Father's House (Birmingham Rep); Hornbills, Absurd Person Singular, Skirmishes, A Midsummer Night's Dream (Leatherhead); Filumena (Bromley); The Vortex, Pride and Prejudice, The Way of the World (CTC); Significant Others, Brighton Beach Memoirs (Coventry); Bedroom Farce (Oxford Playhouse); The Country Wife, Ghosts (Actors Company).

TV includes: In Suspicious Circumstances, Inspector Alleyn, Unnatural Pursuits, Between the Lines, The Fall Out Guy, Put on By Cunning; Lizzie's Pictures, Sam Saturday, London Embassy, Hold the Dream, The Gentle Touch, Sense and Sensibility, Shades of Darkness, Tales of the Unexpected, The Lost Tribe, Gems, Miss Marple.

Films include: Bad Behaviour, Nostradamus.

CHERYL CAMPBELL

Theatre includes: work at Glasgow Citizens Theatre, Watford, Birmingham Rep, Theatr Clywd, The Royal Exchange, Manchester; The Betrayal (Almeida Theatre); Miss Julie (Lyric, Hammersmith & Duke of York's); The Doll's House (SWET Award Best Actress), The Changeling, Misha's Party, Macbeth (RSC); Blanche Dubois in A Streetcar Named Desire (Leicester Haymarket/Regional Theatre Best Actress Award); The Sneeze (Aldwych).

TV includes: Dennis Potter's Pennies from Heaven, Rain on the Roof; Malice Aforethought, Testament of Youth (BAFTA Award Best Actress); Inspector Morse, Centrepoint, The Secret Agent (F.I.P.A. Best Actress Award at Cannes).

Films include: Chariots of Fire, Greystoke, The Shooting Party.

NANCY CRANE

Recent theatre includes: Angels in America: Perestroika, The Millenium Approaches (Royal National Theatre); A Walk on Lake Erie (Finborough Theatre); Threesome (Drill Hall & tour); Oh Hell (Lyric, Hammersmith); The Last of the Red Hot Lovers (Derby Playhouse); Caligula (Boulevard Theatre); Never the Sinner (Belgrade Theatre).

Recent TV includes: Last Days of Patton, 92 Grosvenor Street.

Recent films include: The Fourth Protocol.

NICHOLAS FARRELL

Theatre includes: Walpurgis Night (The Gate); Kean (Old Vic & Toronto); The Cherry Orchard (Aldwych Theatre); Divine Gossip, Three Sisters, Cymbeline, The Revenger's Tragedy, The Merchant of Venice, Julius Caesar, Red Noses, Desert Air, Hamlet (RSC); Camille (RSC & Comedy Theatre); Crime & Punishment (Lyric, Hammersmith); Anyone for Denis (Whitehall Theatre); Lonestar/Private Wars (Bush); Fears & Misery of the Third Reich (Open Space).

TV includes: The Choir, A Breed of Heroes, To Play the King, The Riff Raff Element, Lipstick on Your Collar, More than a Touch of Zen, Dead Lucky, The Fools on the Hill, Mansfield Park, The White Guard, The Jewel in the Crown.

Films include: Playing Away, Berlin Tunnel 21, Chariots of Fire, Greystoke, The Rocking Horse Winner.

CAROLINE HARKER

For the Royal Court: The Editing Process.

Other theatre includes: Don Juan, Sweet Charity, Daisy Pulls It Off (Harrogate Theatre); Hidden Laughter (Michael Codron Production); The Mongrel's Heart (Royal Lyceum, Edinburgh).

TV includes: Chancer, Casualty, Growing Rich, three series of A Touch of Frost, Riders, Covington Cross, Honey for Tea, Celia in Middlemarch.

Films include: The Madness of George III.

Radio includes: A.S. Byatt's Still Life and Virgin in the Garden, The Swish of the Curtain, Golden Pavements, Losing Contact.

DEIRDRE HARRISON

For the Royal Court: Awake (rehearsed reading), Unidentified Human Remains and the Nature of Love (rehearsed reading).

Other theatre includes: Two Tigers (Edinburgh Festival); Life Under Water (Soho Poly); Don Juan, Sweet Charity (Harrogate Theatre); Little Shop of Horrors, The Iceman Cometh (Lyric, Belfast); You Never Can Tell (West Yorkshire Playhouse); Convictions (Croydon Warehouse); A Slight Case of Murder (Nottingham Playhouse); Angels Still Falling (Boulevard); June Moon (Hampstead & Vaudeville Theatre); The House of Yes (Gate Theatre).

American theatre includes: Act I Company (Williamstown Festival); Bremen Freedom, The Gut Girls (Cucaracha/New York); Three Postcards (Portland Stage Co); Measure for Measure (New Jersey Shakespeare Festival); Leonce and Lena, Threepenny Opera, In the Image of Kings (Yale University).

TV includes: Mystique, 34,000 Steps, London's Burning, Jeeves and Wooster.

Films include: Shining Through, Notorious, Flodder Does Manhattan, Merely Players.

Recording: Psycho Derelict for Pete Townsend.

TOBIAS HOHEISEL (designer)

Theatre & opera designs include: Salome (Teatro Muncipal Rio de Janeiro); Idomeneo (Staatsoper Wien); Der Freischutz (Deutsche Oper Berlin); The Seagull (Schillertheater Berlin); Der Ferne Klang (Theatre de la Monnaie, Brussels); Die Stunde da Wir (Wiener Festwochen); La Boheme (ENO); Orpheus (Deutsche Staatsoper Berlin); Stuetzen der Gesellschaft by Ibsen (Theatre Basel).

Collaborations with Brigitte Fassbaender (Amsterdam) & Anja Silja (on her first mise en scene Lohengrin in Brussels).

Festivals includes: Drottningholm Festival (Sweden); Bregenzer Festspiele (Austria); Katya Kabanova, Jenufa, Death in Venice (Glyndebourne Festival).

Future plans include: Puccini's Il Trittico (La Monnaie, Brussels); Janacek's The Makropoulos Case (Glyndebourne).

NICHOLAS LE PREVOST

For the Royal Court: The Glad Hand, The Last Supper, Seven Lears, Golgo, Eastern Promises.

Recent theatre includes: An Absolute Turkey (Peter Hall Company at the Globe/won Equity's Clarence Derwent Award, nominated for Olivier Award for Best Comedy Performance); The Europeans, Blues for Mister Charlie (Manchester Royal Exchange/ nominated for Manchester Evening News Best Actor Award).

Founder member of the Wrestling School.

Recent TV includes: The Vicar of Dibley, Up the Garden Path, Harnessing Peacocks, The Great Paperchase.

Recent films include: Letters from the East (to be released spring 1995).

Recent radio includes: Victory, Three Men in a Boat, Journey to the Centre of the Earth, In the Red.

Opera includes: Ariadne on Naxos (ENO).

PETER MUMFORD (lighting designer)

Recent lighting designs include: Wallenstein, Ion (RSC); School for Wives (Almeida); Sleeping Beauty (Scottish Ballet); Fearful Symmetries (Royal Ballet); Fidelio (Scottish Opera); Mirandolina (Lyric, Hammersmith); The Yeoman of the Guard (Welsh National Opera); The Compleat Consort (Munich Ballet); The Glass Blew In (Siobhan Davies Dance Company); Passage, Banter Banter (Rambert Dance Company).

He directed the opera The Man Who Strides the Wind for Almeida Opera '93.

Work as a director for TV includes: Strong Language, White Man Sleeps and Wyoming for Dance on Four (CH4); Heaven Ablaze in his Breast, Dancehouse, Five Dances by Martha Graham and White Bird Featherless (BBC2); Natural Selection (BBC Wales); Cosi fan tutte (La Sept/Arte).

Future work will include lighting design for Simon Boccanegra (Munich Opera); Edward II (Stuttgart Ballet); The Marriage of Figaro (Sydney Opera House); The Winter Guest (Almeida) and a new work for the Siobhan Davies Dance Co.

PATRICK O'KANE

Theatre includes: Observe the Sons of Ulster Marching Towards the Somme, Cat on a Hot Tin Roof (Lyric, Belfast); Donny Boy, Julius Caesar, Absurd Person Singular (Manchester Royal Exchange); The Plough and the Stars (Abbey Theatre); Playboy of the Western World, 1953, Lulu, Edward II, Sweet Bird of Youth (Glasgow Citizens); Blood Wedding (Lyric, Hammersmith & tour); The Life of Stuff (Donmar Warehouse); The Grapes of Wrath, The Three Musketeers (Sheffield Crucible).

TV includes: A Safe House, Fair City, Rides, Pie in the Sky.

Films include: The Paris Express.

Radio: The Rover.

WILLIAM OSBORNE

Theatre includes: Our Day Out, Christmas Carol (Nottingham Playhouse); Joseph and the Amazing Technicolour Dreamcoat (Leicester Haymarket); As You Like It (Manchester Royal Exchange & tour); Pravda, Hobson's Choice, All's Well That Ends Well (Leeds Playhouse); Rough Crossing (tour); Paris Match (Theatr Clwyd); Screamers (Arts Theatre); The Secret Agent (Etcetera); The Last Enemy (Drill Hall); The Case of the Frightened Lady (Palace, Watford); The Deep Blue Sea (Almeida & Apollo); The Rivals (Chichester Festival & Albery).

TV includes: Have his Carcase, Rumpole of the Bailey, Victoria Wood Playhouse, Poirot, Absolute Hell, Don't Leave Me This Way, Look At It This Way, Victoria Wood Christmas Special, Pie in the Sky, Fall from Grace, Cold Comfort Farm.

Films include: Damage, Tom and Viv.

JOHN PADDEN

For the Royal Court: Six Degrees of Separation (& Comedy Theatre).

Other theatre includes: Doctor Knock, The Case of Rebellious Susan (Orange Tree); She Stoops to Conquer (West End & tour); The Coal Dust Affair (ATC); Bad Blood (Gate Theatre); Marching Song (Theatr Clwyd).

TV includes: Martin Chuzzlewit.

Radio: Bad Blood.

STEVEN PIMLOTT (director)

Steven Pimlott has directed for the Royal National Theatre, Moliere's The Miser and Sondheim's Sunday in the Park with George - nominated for an Olivier award. For the Royal Shakespeare Company Julius Caeser, Murder in the Cathedral, Measure for Measure and a new play by Michael Hastings Unfinished Business. For English National Opera La Boheme. For the Almeida Butterfly Kiss by Phyllis Nagy. His arena production of Carmen has been seen in London, Dortmund, Tokyo, Melbourne, Sydney, Zurich, Munich and Berlin. He was nominated for an Olivier award for his production of Joseph and the Amazing Colour Dreamcoat in the Wets End, currently playing in Chicago. He has directed more than thirty productions of opera in the U.K, Germany, Austria, Austrailia and Israel. Other musical productions include the British premiere of Carmen Jones and a revival of Carousel.

Future plans include Vieux Carre by Tennessee Williams at Nottingham Playhouse, and Richard III for the Royal Shakespeare Company.

The Royal Court Theatre are grateful to the following for their support of this production:

Wardrobe care by Persil and Comfort courtesy of Lever Brothers Ltd, watches by The Timex Corporation, refrigerators by Electrolux and Philips Major Appliances Ltd.; kettles for rehearsals by Morphy Richards; video for casting purposes by Hitachi; backstage coffee machine by West 9; furniture by Knoll International; freezer for backstage use supplied by Zanussi Ltd 'Now that's a good idea.' Hair by Carole at Edmond's, 19 Beauchamp Place, SW3. Closed circuit TV cameras and monitors by Mitsubishi UK Ltd. Natural spring water from Wye Spring Water, 149 Sloane Street, London SW1, tel. 071-730 6977. Overhead projector from W.H. Smith.

HOW THE ROYAL COURT IS BROUGHT TO YOU...

The English Stage Company at the Royal Court Theatre is supported financially by a wide range of public bodies and private companies, as well as its own trading activities. The theatre receives its principal funding from the **Arts Council of England**, which has supported the Royal Court since 1956. The **Royal Borough of Kensington & Chelsea** gives an annual grant to the Royal Court Young People's Theatre and provides some of its staff. The **London Boroughs Grants Committee** contributes to the cost of productions in the Theatre Upstairs.

Other parts of the Royal Court's activities are made possible by business sponsorships. Several of these sponsors have made a long term commitment. 1995 sees the fifth Barclays New Stages Festival of Independent Theatre, which has been supported throughout by **Barclays Bank**. **British Gas North Thames** has so far supported three years of the Royal Court's Education Programme. Now in its 22nd year, the Young Writers' Festival has been sponsored by **Marks & Spencer** since 1991. The latest sponsorship by **WH Smith** has been to help make the launch of the new Friends of the Royal Court scheme so successful.

We are particularly grateful to the **Audrey Skirball - Kenis Theatre** of Los Angeles for providing funding to support a series of work new to the Main Stage, including so far Jonathan Harvey's **BABIES**, and Meredith Oakes' **THE EDITING PROCESS**. 1993 saw the start of our association with the Audrey Skirball-Kenis Theatre. The Skirball Foundation is funding a Playwrights Programme at the Royal Court. Exchange visits for writers between Britain and the USA complement the greatly increased programme of readings and workshops which have fortified the Royal Court's capability to develop new plays.

The much expanded season of plays in the Theatre Upstairs by young new writers would not have been possible without the generous sponsorship of the **Jerwood Foundation**. The season is being produced in association with the **Royal National Theatre Studio**.

In 1988 the Royal Court launched the **Olivier Building Appeal** to raise funds to restore, repair and improve the theatre building. So far nearly £750,000 has been raised. The theatre has new bars and front of house areas, new roofs, air conditioning and central heating boilers, a rehearsal room and a completely restored and cleaned facade. This would not have been possible without a very large number of generous supporters and significant contributions from the **Theatres' Restoration Fund**, the **Rayne Foundation**, the **Foundation for Sport and the Arts** and the **Arts Council's Incentive Funding Scheme**.

The **Gerald Chapman Award** was founded in 1988 to train and develop young theatre directors. It is now jointly funded by the Royal Court and **BBC Television.** The **ITV Companies** fund the **Regional Theatre Young Directors Scheme**, with which the Royal Court has been associated for many years.

The Royal Court earns the rest of the money it needs to operate from the Box Office, from other trading and from the transfers of plays such as **Death and the Maiden, Six Degrees of Separation, Oleanna** and currently **My Night With Reg** to the West End. But without public subsidy it would close immediately and its unique place in British Theatre would be lost. If you care about the future of arts in this country, please write to your MP and say so.

PATRONS
Christopher Bland
Diana Bliss
Henny Gestetner OBE
John Mortimer
Richard Pulford
Sir George Russell
Richard Wilson
Irene Worth

CORPORATE PATRONS
Advanpress
Associated Newspapers Ltd
BMI Healthcare
Bunzl PLC
Caradon plc
Carlton Communications
Compass Group plc
Criterion Productions plc
CS First Boston Ltd
Freshfields
Gardner Merchant Ltd
Homevale Ltd
Laporte plc
Lazard Brothers and Co Ltd
Lex Services PLC
The Mirror Group PLC

New Penny Productions Ltd
Penguin Books Ltd
The Simkins Partnership
Simons Muirhead and Burton
Tomkins plc
Touch Ross & Co.
Vodafone Group

ASSOCIATES
Robyn Durie
Nicholas A Fraser
Kingsmead Charitable Trust
Patricia Marmont
Barbara Minto
Peter Jones

BENEFACTORS
Mr &Mrs G Acher
James R Beery
Mrs Denise Bouché
Carole & Neville Conrad
Conway Van Gelder
David Coppard & Co
Coppings Trust
Curtis Brown Ltd
Allan Davis
Robert Dufton
D M M Dutton
D T Dutton
Anthony M Fry
Maggi Gordon
Murray Gordon
Rocky Gottlieb
Granada Television Ltd
Romaine Hart
Andre Hoffman
Jarvis Hotels Ltd
Peter Job
Lady Lever
Ian Martin
Pat Morton
T J Norris
Michael Orr
Eric Parker
Pearson plc
Paola Piglia
Angharad Rees
Rentokil Group plc
Sears plc
Nicholas Selmes
Lord Sheppard
Swiss Bank Corporation
William Morris Agency

THE OLIVIER BUILDING APPEAL

The Royal Court reached the ripe old age of 100 in September 1988. The theatre was showing its age somewhat, and the centenary was celebrated by the launch of the Olivier Appeal, to repair and improve the building.

Laurence Olivier's long association with the Court began as a schoolboy. He was given "a splendid seat in the Dress Circle" to see his first Shakespeare, *Henry IV Part 2* and was later to appear as Malcolm in *Macbeth* (in modern dress) in a Barry Jackson production, visiting from the Birmingham Repertory Theatre in 1928. His line of parts also included the Lord in the Prologue of *The Taming of the Shrew*. This early connection and his astonishing return in *The Entertainer,* which changed the direction of his career in 1957, made it natural that he should be the Appeal Patron. After his death, Joan Plowright CBE, the Lady Olivier, consented to take over as Patron.

With the generous gifts of our many friends and donors, notably The Rayne Foundation, and an award from the Arts Council's Incentive Fund, we have enlarged and redecorated the bars and front of house areas, installed a new central heating boiler and new air conditioning equipment in both theatres, rewired many parts of the building, redecorated the dressing rooms and we are gradually upgrading the lighting and sound equipment.

With the help of the Theatre Restoration Fund, work has now been completed on building a rehearsal room and replacing the ancient roofs. The Foundation for Sport and the Arts provided a grant which enabled us to restore the faded Victorian facade of the theatre. So, much is being done, but much remains to do, to replace our ancient wooden grid and antequated flying system, and to improve the technical facilities backstage which will open up new possibilities for our set designers.

Can you help? A tour of the theatre, including its more picturesque parts, can be arranged by ringing Catherine King on *0171 730 5174*. If you would like to help with an event or a gift please ring Graham Cowley, General Manager, on the same number.
'Secure the Theatre's future, and take it forward towards the new century. For the health of the whole theatrical life of Britain it is essential that this greatly all-providing theatre we love so much and wish so well continues to prosper.'
Laurence Olivier (1988)

Laurence Olivier 1907-1989
Photo: Snowdon

THE ROYAL COURT THEATRE

THE STRIP

a play by

Phyllis Nagy

As always, for Mel

Characters:

The Americans

AVA COO, mid-to-late 20s.

TINA COO, 45ish.

LESTER MARQUETTE, 40s.

LORETTA MARQUETTE, 30s.

KATE BUCK, mid-30s.

The English

OTTO MINK, alias Murphy Greene, of indeterminate age.

CALVIN HIGGINS, late 20s.

MARTIN HIGGINS, 30ish.

TOM WARNER, early 20s.

SUZY BRADFIELD, 30ish.

The time is the present, shortly before a total solar eclipse.

The setting is a fluid, non-naturalistic landscape dominated by an enormous three-dimensional re-creation of Sphinx and pyramid which represents the exterior of the Luxor Hotel, Las Vegas, Nevada. It never leaves the stage.

Scenes should begin and end in overlap; that is, except where indicated there is never a blackout and the action of those on stage is continuous. It is possible that the physical action of any scene begins before its preceeding scene ends, and so on.

This text went to press before the opening night and may therefore differ from the version as performed.

Act One

Darkness. Music in: 'Rescue Me' (Madonna). Lights up on tableaux, a slow unravelling of scenes:

MARTIN *and* TOM *in their Earls Court flat.* MARTIN *wears scanty workout clothes. He performs an impressive aerobics routine.* TOM *eats chocolate and times* MARTIN *with a stop watch.*

AVA, CALVIN *and* OTTO *at the Chateau L'Amour, Jericho (Long Island).* AVA *tries to look like Madonna. She doesn't. She lip-synchs to the song.* OTTO *and* CALVIN *are reticent.*

SUZY *in her Earls Court flat watching telly, eating crisps and masturbating simultaneously.*

KATE *at her desk in Arlington, Virginia. She wears Walkman headphones. She cleans a 9mm. automatic pistol.*

LESTER *and* LORETTA *in their Earls Court hotel. Their room directly overlooks* MARTIN *and* TOM's *flat.* LESTER *watches* MARTIN *and* TOM. *He polishes a pair of cowboy boots.* LORETTA *bottle feeds her infant son,* RAY. RAY *wears a white miniature Ku Klux Klan hooded robe.*

TINA *in Vegas at a one-arm bandit. She drops coin after coin into the slot without results. She swigs big shots from a bottle of Tequila. She's fairly bored with all of this.*

The music fades into the sudden sound of a progressive slot machine jackpot being hit. Bells and sirens. A river of coins dropping out of slots. The sound is overwhelming.

Everybody listens to the phantom jackpot hit.

Abrupt shift in focus to OTTO, AVA *and* CALVIN *at the Chateau L'Amour.* OTTO *speaks in a deep, wonderfully resonant English voice.* AVA's *a native New Yorker.*

OTTO. Female impersonation is a rather curious career choice for a woman, Miss Coo.

AVA. You could tell? I saw you could tell. I practise too much. Or maybe not enough.

OTTO. I shouldn't have thought rehearsal an issue.

AVA. You're English.

OTTO. Am I?

AVA. I could tell. Hey. We're even. You could tell I was a woman. I could tell you weren't American.

OTTO. But I am American, Miss Coo. I have a passport.

OTTO *displays his passport for* AVA.

AVA. Otto Mink. Is that an English name?

OTTO. No. It's not.

AVA. I always wanted a passport because they're glamorous things to have. Well. Not that I have anywhere glamorous to go. I mean, you don't need a passport to get to the city.

OTTO. Which city?

AVA. You know. *The* city.

OTTO. Yes. I see your point.

AVA. Anyway, my mother used to say, Ava darling, tits are the only passport a girl will ever need.

OTTO *puts away his passport.*

OTTO. Miss Coo. I will be frank. Your act is not appropriate for the Chateau L'Amour.

AVA. Okay, well, fair's fair.

OTTO. You are talentless.

AVA. Oh. Do you – I mean – is there, like a reason you carry your passport with you? Because I never met anybody else who did that and I was just wondering, well, do you think I could ever be –

OTTO. Citizenship is precious, Miss Coo.

AVA. Maybe I'm mediocre? Is that what you mean?

OTTO. No.

AVA. Your passport picture is good, Mr. Mink. Usually they cut off the top of your head or they catch you drooling and your hair looks like Little Richard's. I know about hair. I've got a certificate from the Wilfred Academy of Beauty. Two years, it took me. Turns out I'm allergic to hair spray. Two fucking years.

OTTO. Many of us take decades before finding our vocations.

AVA. I don't really look like a girl. I'm too . . . something. I got big tits, but they look fake, or so this guy from Hoboken told me. I went to beauty school with this drag queen, Tina, and I think I kind of look like her so . . . so. It was this or Star Search. I figure, the t.v. camera doesn't lie but maybe a smoky scuzzy club full of drunken queens will. That's my mother's name. Tina. Funny, ain't it?

OTTO. Perhaps if your mother was a drag queen.

AVA. I have performed my act in public. I want you to know that. People paid to see me.

OTTO. The Chateau L'Amour is not a smoky scuzzy club, Miss Coo.

AVA. Hey, wait, I didn't mean – I'm sorry. I speak just total . . . shit. Oh God. Why can't I just want to be a typist or an actress like normal women?

OTTO. Because you're idiosyncratic. Special.

AVA. Yeah. Talentless jerkoff me. Real special.

OTTO. Talent is a liability in the most important jobs.

AVA. Oh sure. Tell that to, you know, Steven fucking Spielberg.

OTTO. I speak of true importance. Relevance. Resonance. For instance: are saints talented?

AVA. What – you mean, like the chick who went crazy and ate clay or or – the guy who talked to birds? My mother has this gigantic book of saints, with pictures and – you know who my favourite one is? Veronica. What a fantastic name. And her picture. Terrific makeup. She wore the most beautiful shade of blue eye shadow.

OTTO. Exactly. Do you think Saint Veronica had any talent?
Or Saints Theresa, Bernadette and Anthony, for that matter?

AVA. Sure. Of course they had talent. They did things like . . .
shit. They did miracles.

OTTO. No, Miss Coo. They had a calling. A common vocation.
The hand of God provided their direction. They were empty
vessels waiting to be filled with relevance.

AVA. Jesus. Well. That's depressing.

OTTO. Just as you are an empty vessel waiting for me to fill
you.

AVA. Uh-huh. Okay. I'm . . . open. To suggestion.

OTTO. I own another club. The club is located in another part
of this country. I will write its name down on this slip of
paper. You will take the slip of paper.

OTTO *produces, as if from nowhere, a pad and pen. He
scribbles on a piece of paper. He holds it out to* AVA.

OTTO. Take it.

AVA *takes the piece of paper. She stares at it.*

AVA. Tumbleweed Junction. Okay. So.

OTTO. Find it and sing, Miss Coo. Good luck.

OTTO *prepares to leave.*

AVA. Hey, wait. Is there something you're forgetting to tell
me, like, where this club is and maybe how I'm supposed to
get there? I mean, I got a car but where the hell am I
supposed to be driving it? And – correct me if I'm wrong
here – but are you offering me a job, Mr. Mink?

OTTO. All the information you need is written on that slip of
paper.

AVA. Oh great. Two words. Two fucking words. Tumbleweed
Junction. Hey – this ain't in Jersey, is it? I'm not singing in
Jersey. (*Referring to* CALVIN.) Maybe your friend here
knows the directions?

OTTO. I've never seen this man before.

OTTO *exits.*

AVA. Find it and sing. My ass.

CALVIN (*he's English, but he's lived in America for a long time and has no perceptible English accent*). I loved your act. It made me cry.

AVA. You cried? Nah. You didn't cry. Did you?

CALVIN. Yes. I did. I cry at odd times.

AVA. Hey. If he don't know you, you don't work here. Right.

CALVIN. Right. I don't work here.

AVA. You ever hear of a club called Tumbleweed Junction? I bet it's some dive in Secaucus. I just know it.

CALVIN. Sorry. No. I don't go to clubs much. But I . . . I think you are talented. And I couldn't tell that you were a woman.

AVA. That's . . . really nice of you to say.

CALVIN. My brother's gay.

AVA. Oh. Really.

CALVIN. It sounds strange to tell you, I know, but I have been to clubs with him where female impersonators have performed. So I know. A little something. About it. (*Beat.*) That was long ago, of course.

AVA. Sure. Uhm . . . I gotta get a map of America, 'cause it looks like I'm taking a trip. You don't by any chance have a road map? Or a twenty for some gas? I'm broke.

CALVIN. I do. Have a map, that is. Would you like it?

CALVIN *takes a map out of his back pocket and gives it to* AVA.

AVA. Thanks. I . . . hey. If you don't work in this club, why are you here?

CALVIN. I'm English, too. Like the owner of this club. I don't know exactly where he's from, but it's someplace southern. And wealthy. I've been here a long time. Too long. Anyway, that's why I don't have an accent. I'm Calvin. Calvin Higgins.

CALVIN *and* AVA *shake hands.*

AVA. Ava Coo. Answer my question. What are you doing here?

CALVIN. What an unusual name. Ava. Coo. Lovely. Soft.

AVA. Yeah. I'm named after a French murderess.

CALVIN. You're joking.

AVA. I'm not. Answer my question, Calvin.

CALVIN. I'm looking for you.

AVA. That's a really tired line. And I remember asking if you could lend me a twenty for gas. I got places to get to.

CALVIN. Well. That's just it, Ava Coo. I'm here to repossess your car.

Shift to LESTER *and* LORETTA *in their Earls Court hotel room.* LESTER *obsessively polishes and repolishes his cowboy boots throughout the scene.* LORETTA *holds* BABY RAY. *She reads very slowly and deliberately to* RAY *from a book. Both* LESTER *and* LORETTA *speak in quite broad Virginia (southern) accents.*

LORETTA. 'What did they look like? Early Romans came from a tribe called the Latins. Latins had olive skin and dark hair. When their empire spread across Europe, other people began to settle in Rome. As time went on, the Romans included people with lots of different looks.' (*Beat.*) I'm not sure I like this book, Lester.

LESTER. Baby Ray's a leader. Leaders learn about everything, beginning with the Romans.

LORETTA. The Romans weren't olive skinned. They were white.

LESTER. I know that, Loretta. You don't got to tell me. And I don't think the book is suggesting that the Romans weren't white. The book is saying that the Romans were Italians.

LORETTA. If you say so. (*She continues to read.*) 'Romans had many more baths and were a lot cleaner than people in other ancient civilisations. Both men and women loved wearing expensive perfume.' There is something wrong with this book, Lester. I will not have Baby Ray believing that it's right for men to wear expensive perfumes.

LESTER. That ain't the point of the story, Loretta. You got no appreciation for the great cultures. But that doesn't mean Baby Ray ain't gonna have any.

LORETTA. Well, what is the point of the story then, Lester? That the Romans were cleaner than everybody else?

LESTER. Yeah. That's it.

LORETTA. Where did you get this book?

LESTER. Cleanliness is next to Godliness.

LORETTA. We take showers, Lester. I change Baby Ray's diaper seventeen times a day. Believe me. I know all about cleanliness.

LESTER. All I'm saying is, if you find out who the cleanest people are, they are always the smartest people.

LORETTA. Such as?

LESTER. Shit, Loretta. Why do you got to bother me when I'm cleaning my boots? Why do you do this to me, woman?

LORETTA. Such as? I am waiting for an example, Lester. Mr. Mink says we learn by example.

LESTER. For example. The Swiss. They are very clean. They are first class inventors. The Germans. They're so clean, they all have blond eyelashes. Smartest people in the world. Have I proved my point?

LORETTA. Only northern Germans are clean.

LESTER. Who told you that?

LORETTA. I read. I put two and two together.

LESTER. Why don't you just . . . read some more to Baby Ray. He's got to know about the Romans.

LORETTA. Fact: northerners everywhere are always cleaner. Look at America. Need I go on?

LESTER. I swear you don't know your ass from a hole in the ground. Remember where we live?

LORETTA. Virginia is not the south. Virginia is a rich state.

Always has been. And we don't live in Roanoke anymore, Lester. We live in a bed and breakfast in goddamned Earls Court in the goddamned United Kingdom. Get used to it.

LESTER. We ain't gonna be clean for long. There's no shower.

LORETTA. Adapt to circumstance. Assimilate. Conquer. Mr. Mink's triple crown for success.

LESTER. Fuck you, Loretta. I'm not sitting in my own dirt.

LORETTA. The Roman generals took baths.

LESTER. They had no choice. There was no electricity or water pressure.

LORETTA. You talk shit, Lester. And I am not sitting in this hotel room like I'm some kind of prisoner. I am going out to see what I can see.

LESTER. You can't do that, Loretta. You will not do that. We are waiting on Mr. Mink's call.

LORETTA. Three days and three nights. It's time to go, Lester.

LESTER. Jesus waited forty days and forty nights.

LORETTA. Jesus was in the desert, Lester, not London. There wasn't restaurants or entertainment available.

LESTER. We wait for his call. Anyway, what do you think you're gonna see out there?

LORETTA. Sights.

LESTER. There's a couple of homos living across the airshaft. One of them dances around with weights, the other one eats. Go out. See the sights, Loretta.

LORETTA. You don't got to look at it. See no evil.

LESTER. You really ain't the smartest person in the world.

LORETTA. No, Lester, I'm not the smartest. But I am the best person for you. And do you know why I am the best person for you? Because I believe that you are the smartest person in the world. Because I believe that *you* will be famous and in the process, you will make me a very rich woman. And when I am a very rich woman, I will send Baby Ray off to Oxford and I will eat Belgian chocolates until I am the fattest, most docile wife a man could hope for. I will be so fat, you will have to build extension after extension to our Georgian mansion. And then, Lester, I will be truly happy and I won't ask you another question about the Romans or about why I am cooped up in some dump of a hotel without a shower or why it is we no longer have a home.

LESTER. I'm already famous.

LORETTA. You're a fugitive. I don't think that qualifies.

LESTER. You're a fugitive with me.

LORETTA. No way. I didn't do nothing but slip a ring on my finger and give birth to your child.

The telephone rings. It rings again. And again. LESTER *answers. He listens. He hangs up.*

LESTER. Looks like we'll be testing out one of your finer sociological theories. We're going north.

Shift to TINA *on her hands and knees at the Tumbleweed Junction, Las Vegas. She uses a scrub-brush to clean the floor with one hand, and holds a small Dictaphone in the other hand. Distant sound of slot machines, roulette wheels.* TINA *speaks into the Dictaphone.*

TINA. Dear Ava. I probably didn't get your last letter because when I married Mr. Marshall, I moved house. Not that my split level wasn't nice enough for us but . . . well now I live on a one-hundred and fifty acre ranch with Mr. Marshall. And before that, I was so busy at the casino I was hardly ever home to get my mail. But I know you wrote to me, Ava. And I know what you wrote about because let's face it honey, all our letters say the same thing. The weather is good, the weather is bad, and so on. I put pen to paper and I find myself writing the same old things, who knows why. So I am sending you a tape in the hope that it will change our routine. Mr. Marshall gave me this Dictaphone as a wedding gift and you know I've always been a freer talker than a writer. You would like Mr. Marshall. He's tall and rarely speaks. But he opens doors for me and buys me bunches of daisies from the Seven-Eleven and really, Ava, that's more than good enough. I miss your voice, honey. It's hard being a casino supervisor in Vegas, but it's rewarding. As you can imagine, I don't make many friends on the gaming floor, but I am a fair boss and last week I got Dolly Parton's autograph. Mr. Marshall breeds horses. I keep an eye out for promising colts. So far there's no hint of a Secretariat, but his horses are strong and good looking. Like him. I am babbling and so I better get to the point of this letter which is: I think I saw your daddy's picture in a newspaper last week. I say I think it was him because I haven't seen him in twenty years but it looked just like him. Except in the newspapers his name was Marquette and he looked much thinner than when I knew him. I think he killed twenty-seven people at a truck stop in Lynchburg. Well. That's all for now. I hope you are still enjoying success as a cabaret singer. I am so proud of you, Ava. With love, your mother, Mrs. Tina Coo Marshall.

The casino sounds suddenly grow much louder, as OTTO *enters. And then, just as suddenly, the sounds drop down to their previous level.*

OTTO. Mrs. Marshall. A pleasure, as always.

TINA. You're not supposed to be in here, Mr. Greene. This is the ladies room.

OTTO. I do own this establishment.

TINA. Yeah but . . . it's weird, you being in here.

OTTO. This is my ladies room, Mrs. Marshall. And you are my primary lady.

TINA. Oh Mr. Greene. You shouldn't flirt.

OTTO. I'm not.

TINA. We're, uhm, running out of extra strength Lysol.

OTTO. Are we?

TINA. I had to bring some from home today. Will we be getting it on delivery any time soon?

OTTO. I'm afraid not.

TINA. Oh. Well. But how can I clean the toilets without it?

OTTO. Be inventive, Mrs. Marshall. Employee initiative brings its own reward.

TINA. We ran out of rubber gloves last week.

OTTO. I'm aware of that.

TINA. I could use a raise. The plumbing in my trailer's been busted for months and you don't know how tired I am of taking sponge baths here. I can't get my clothes clean. They don't fit too good in these tiny sinks and my sweaters got soapy residue all over them. I itch all the time, Mr. Greene.

OTTO. Have you heard from Mr. Marshall lately?

TINA. Not exactly.

OTTO. These are hard times. We must make do with what we have.

TINA. What if we got nothing?

OTTO. Why is your glass always half empty, Mrs. Marshall, and never half full?

TINA. Because I drink a lot.

OTTO. Have you finished with my Dictaphone?

TINA. Oh sure, I was just . . . you ever notice how when you play back a tape your voice doesn't sound like your voice?

OTTO. I've had complaints from several guests. The loos aren't clean enough. The lavatory floor is grimy. There are standards to be upheld at Tumbleweed Junction, Mrs. Marshall. Who hasn't been working hard enough?

TINA. I need this job. Please let me keep my job.

OTTO. Who hasn't been working hard enough?

TINA. There's not another hotel in town that'll hire me. I'm trying to get a place at croupier school but they won't take me until I got some hotel experience. And no hotel will take me on unless I got experience at one of the big places. God. I wanna work at the Luxor, Mr. Greene. I wanna know what it's like inside that pyramid.

OTTO. Just tell me. Who hasn't been working hard enough?

TINA. I . . . me. Me. I haven't been working hard enough.

OTTO. What happens when we don't work hard enough?

TINA. We get docked. I get docked.

OTTO *takes the Dictaphone away from* TINA.

OTTO. Thank you, Mrs. Marshall. I believe a day's wages will be sufficient.

OTTO *holds out his hand to* TINA.

TINA. You want me to give you one day's pay. Now?

OTTO. Why not? What you no longer have can't hurt you.

TINA *digs some cash out of her shoe and gives it to* OTTO.

TINA. I don't understand you a lot of the time, Mr. Greene. But I thank Christ you don't fire me.

OTTO. I'm inscrutable. Like the Sphinx.

TINA *resumes scrubbing the floor.*

TINA. Whatever. (*Beat.*) My husband's a trucker. It's not unusual that I don't hear from him say, for a few weeks. Or months.

OTTO *removes the tape from the Dictaphone. He bends down to give* TINA *the tape.*

OTTO. You shouldn't spend so much time on your knees, Mrs. Marshall. It's bad for the circulation.

Shift to MARTIN *and* TOM *in their Earls Court flat.* MARTIN *sits on a straight-back chair. He wears only jockey briefs.* TOM *bathes* MARTIN's *feet. He uses an old-fashioned foot basin and a pitcher of water.* SUZY *does sit-ups. She's not expert.*

SUZY. So I run this bloke's details through the software programme. He's a Gemini with Gemini rising and a moon in Capricorn. A complete mess. He's a bankrupt, his boyfriend's fucked off with a Chippendale and to make things worse, the bloody computer tells me he's got eight months to live. I don't know what to do. I mean, do I write to him and say, awfully sorry, but you have no future?

MARTIN. Pouf.

SUZY. That's not very nice. He isn't dying because he's a pouf.

MARTIN. No, Suzy. You're a pouf. You do sit-ups like a pouf.

TOM. You're a pouf, Martin. You do sit-ups.

MARTIN. Shut up. (*Beat*.) Computer astrology software does not predict the future.

SUZY. Mine does. Don't ask me how. But it does.

MARTIN. That's impossible.

TOM. I've seen it work. Once I watched while Suzy ran an entire sixth form –

MARTIN. This water's tepid.

TOM. I'll fetch some hot. I'm sorry.

MARTIN. Never mind.

SUZY stops doing sit-ups. TOM continues to bathe MARTIN's feet.

SUZY. Anyway, I've been taking on too many mail-order jobs. Last month I got a letter from a very strange woman in America. Real nutter. A journalist . . . or something. She keeps writing. I think she has me confused with a lonely hearts' club.

TOM. How do you know she's a nutter if you've never met her?

SUZY. You can tell from a letter.

TOM. I couldn't.

MARTIN. You couldn't tell much now, could you Tommy? (*Beat*.) You ought to do three sets of fifteen, Suzy. And what about those press-ups?

SUZY. I'm knackered, Martin. Really.

MARTIN. Pouf.

TOM. Stop saying that.

MARTIN. Why? Why should I stop?

TOM. Because it bothers me.

A beat, and then MARTIN exits, dripping water everywhere.

TOM. He has a good heart.

SUZY. You should get out more often.

TOM. He misses his brother.

SUZY. Don't be daft. Martin hasn't heard from his brother in years.

TOM. He phoned up. Yesterday.

SUZY. Calvin? You heard from Calvin?

TOM. Said he was in love with a girl called Ava. She's a drag queen. Apparently.

SUZY. And? What else did he have to say for himself?

TOM. Nothing. That was all.

SUZY. You fancy a curry? I do. I'm starved. I gave up waiting for Calvin's letters three years ago. December. The twelfth. Eight a.m. Central heating out. Enough jam for one croissant. Red notice from BT. And I stopped missing Calvin Higgins.

TOM. What will you tell him?

SUZY. Who? What?

TOM. The bloke who's dying.

SUZY. Him. Well. I don't know, do I?

TOM. Tell him the stars suggest a configuration of rare fortune. Tell him he's the most stunning creature alive. Tell him he'll meet a man who will adore him. Who will mend his trousers and his broken heart. Tell it to him over and over.

SUZY *touches her hand to* TOM's *forehead.*

SUZY. You're sweating. Poor Tom.

TOM. Why does he hate me? Why?

SUZY. Why does my astrology software provide me with information nobody else has?

TOM. The stars are strange this month.

SUZY. Come on, then. Teach me a proper press-up.

TOM *demonstrates press-ups for* SUZY. *He does the press-ups very slowly, so she is able to follow his lead.*

TOM. It's really very simple. See.

SUZY. I wish I believed fitness could be fun.

> TOM *suddenly accelerates. He's going very fast and breathing very hard.* SUZY *can't keep up.*

SUZY. Tom. TOM. YOU'RE WHEEZING. THAT'S ENOUGH.

> *But* TOM *doesn't stop. He keeps going.* SUZY *pours the pitcher of water over* TOM'*s head. He stops abruptly, and lets himself fall face down onto the floor.*

TOM.FuckhimfuckhimfuckhimfuckhimFUCKFUCKFUCK HIMHIMHIM.

> SUZY, *at a complete loss, pats* TOM'*s back tentatively.*

SUZY. Okay. Okay. Poor Tom. Okay. Sssh. Sssh. Poor Tom. Okay.

> *Shift to* OTTO *and* KATE *at* KATE'*s office in Arlington, Virginia.* KATE *wears Walkman headphones. She carries a rather large purse.*

KATE. The leads you gave me don't check out.

OTTO. I felt certain they would.

KATE. Well they don't. What do you make of that?

OTTO. I haven't any notion. You are the reporter, Miss Buck. Report.

KATE. I wasn't an investigative reporter, Murphy. I was a columnist. There's a difference.

OTTO. Nonetheless. I hired you as a reporter.

KATE. I can't find Marquette. He's not in Roanoke. He's not anywhere in Virginia. Or in the Carolinas for that matter. Lynchburg cops got a positive ID on the prints found at the truck stop. And they are not Lester Marquette's prints.

OTTO. I believe they are.

KATE. I will not report false information. I have a duty to our readership.

OTTO. The Arlington Pennysaver is not The New York Times, Miss Buck.

KATE. It's still a newspaper. Even if it is a weekly. A free weekly. A free weekly shopper. Oh fuck. Why did I let you hire me?

OTTO. I seem to recall a rather nasty incident involving your ethics at the Philadelphia Inquirer.

KATE. I was duped.

OTTO. Pre-teen calculus genius with a crack habit plus disabled mum equals a prize-winning story. Heartrending. Metaphorical. And a fabrication.

KATE. I WAS DUPED.

OTTO *approaches* KATE. *He lifts up one of* KATE*'s headphone speakers and leans in close to listen to what she's listening to. A beat, before he replaces the headphone in* KATE*'s ear and steps back.*

OTTO. If the fingerprints aren't Lester Marquette's, then to whom do they belong? You said there was a positive identification.

KATE. That's right. It's positively not Lester Marquette.

OTTO. You favour sentimental popular music, Miss Buck.

KATE. I do not. I like . . . a little Motown, a little disco, this and that.

OTTO. The sentimental are always duped. In journalism as in life. I prefer jazz to pop. It resists false notions of a single shared experience and is therefore unsentimental. Your reportage has been flabby of late.

KATE. So I'm supposed to buy a Thelonius Monk tape and that'll fix it? I don't think so. You want to know what my problem is?

OTTO. Not especially.

KATE. I track down leads about some twelve-year-old's stolen Raleigh. I cover the grand openings of, let's see, bingo halls, electrolysis clinics, Weight Watchers. You name it, Murphy. I'm there. I'm hot. Mrs. fucking Esposito's blender disappears: Kate's got a few inches in Community Corner for it. No problem not a problem hey I'm smiling see me smile see me take a photo of this new-born or that blue ribbon Alsatian no problem I'm happy I'm there and I WAS A COLUMNIST GODDAMNIT.

OTTO. Displays of excessive emotion bore me, Miss Buck.

KATE. I'm being watched by a person who lives in another country.

OTTO. Which country?

KATE. I don't know. Another one. Does it matter?

OTTO. I should think it matters a great deal. Canada is relatively nearby. England, on the other hand, is not.

KATE. England. Why do you say England?

Lights up on SUZY. *She works out on an exercise bike while writing a letter.*

OTTO. An obsession with unanswerable questions is the first sign of insanity. Concern yourself with easy answers. Find Lester Marquette and you will have the story of your life.

OTTO *exits. Music in: 'Native New Yorker' (Odyssey).* KATE*'s been listening to this tune on her Walkman. She listens to the song seriously for a moment, then removes a letter from her bag and reads it as she bops along to the music.*

SUZY (*plugging away on the bicycle*). Dear Kate Buck. My advert, which ought to have run in Astrology Monthly, mistakenly ran in Looking for Love, a publication I am not familiar with. My life is a bit of a mess just at the moment so I'm not surprised by odd occurrences. I think it has something to do with the upcoming solar eclipse and also my Mars is in Scorpio, which explains a great deal. But enough about me. Yes, I am interested in holistic healing, crystals, natural childbirth, macrobiotics and the lot, but I am fairly certain that I'm not a lesbian. I mean, I'm always receptive to new experiences. An astrologer has to be. But I have to admit I enjoy a good rogering every once in a while and therefore I feel your letters, however sensitive and entertaining, are quite missing their mark. I'm sorry, but since I've rarely been outside of London, I don't see how I could have been born in New York City. And as your dream date is a native New Yorker, I'm afraid that leaves me out. One of my ex boyfriends lives somewhere near New York City, and he once sent me a miniature Statue of Liberty. But that's as close as I got, since he stopped writing to me shortly afterwards. Though I do thank you for the cassette. I have fond memories of dancing with my gay friend, Martin, to that song in the late seventies. Good luck in your search and I'd appreciate your not writing to me again. Unless, of course, you'd like me to prepare your chart. I'm sure we could agree on a rate. Sincerely, Suzy Bradfield.

Lights down on SUZY. KATE *folds up the letter carefully, kisses it, puts it back in her bag. She removes her 9mm. automatic pistol from the bag and once again begins the ritual of cleaning it. Music out.*

Shift focus to AVA *and* CALVIN *on a street in Arlington, Virginia.* AVA *consults a map.*

CALVIN. We should have headed west, Ava Coo.

AVA. Look. I got sick of you back in Pennsylvania in that that – what the hell was that loony tunes town you dragged me through –

CALVIN. It was an Amish village.

AVA. Yeah, well, they were fucking out to lunch.

CALVIN. I'm interested in the way they live.

AVA. What's to be interested in? They don't have zippers. What kind of people don't have zippers? I'll tell you, Calvin. Wackos. That's who.

CALVIN. They do just as well with buttons, Ava Coo.

AVA. I'm gonna shove a button up your ass if you don't stop calling me Ava Coo like I'm some kind of . . . bug. Ava. A-V-A. Get it?

CALVIN. Yours is a name that begs to be heard in its entirety. Like a Beethoven piano sonata.

AVA. Oh boy. Listen to me Liberace: THIS IS MY TRIP. Okay? It's my trip, it's my car, it's my map and we go where I say we go. And we are going south. As soon as I figure out why my friggin' car won't start.

CALVIN. It's not your car anymore.

AVA. Just . . . why do you do that? Huh? Never got anything
good to say. Always bringing me down.
DownDOWNDOWN.

CALVIN. And actually, it's my map.

AVA. I'm gonna put my fist through your ugly fat face if you
don't SHUT UP about it already. I swear to God those
fruitcake Amish put some kind of fucking hex on me and
my car.

CALVIN. You shouldn't blame others for your own
misfortune.

AVA. You know, you really ought to do some evangelising
'cause you'd make a fortune with this thine neighbour
thyself thou holy shit. (*A beat.*) I shouldn't have laughed at
that Amish kid's pants. I knew they were into that voodoo
hoodoo crap. Shitshit. Where the hell are we?

CALVIN. Arlington, Virginia. President Kennedy's buried
here. Would you like to see his grave?

AVA. Fuck off.

CALVIN. Respect history and it will respect you.

AVA. You're unbelievable. It's like you drop a coin in your
mouth and some stupid saying comes out your ass.

CALVIN. His grave has an eternal flame. I'd like to see it.

AVA. Listen. I wasn't even born when Kennedy, you know,
rest in peace and all that shit, and my mother didn't vote for
him. So go yourself. Bye-bye.

CALVIN. The very thought of an eternal flame fills my heart
with an inexplicable longing. Why don't you feel it?

AVA. You're really freaking me out, Calvin. Why don't you
take the car, okay, take the car and do . . . whatever you
gotta do with it. I'll hitch.

CALVIN. I can't leave you.

AVA. Sure you can. I'm like a doormat. People coming and
going, breaking and entering, the whole time.

CALVIN. I'm sorry, but I'm meant to be with you.

AVA. I'm pretty sure I was meant to be with Paul Newman, but I'm not so.

CALVIN. My face isn't fat. And I'm not ugly. At least I don't think I am. Am I?

AVA. What – okay, no. You're not ugly. I'm sorry.

CALVIN. What about my face? Is it fat? Do you really think it's fat?

AVA. I don't – it's just an expression. Like when you're mad at somebody you say, you know, you say, fuck you, you fat face bastard. Like that.

CALVIN. A figure of speech.

AVA. Yeah. Whatever. (*Beat.*) How many phone books can we go through in how many hick towns looking for some dive that probably doesn't exist?

CALVIN. It exists.

AVA. How do you know? How do you know that Mink guy wasn't pulling my pud? People always pull my pud. I have that kind of face.

CALVIN. You're beautiful.

AVA. All right all right. Don't start up again. I'm warning you.

KATE *enters. She listens to her Walkman intently and dangles the pistol nonchalantly. She's in a world only she understands and therefore doesn't notice* AVA *and* CALVIN.

AVA. Ohmygod I've read about this kind of right wing southern lunatic with a gun. Ohmygod we're gonna die.

CALVIN. She's just . . . walking. Thinking. Relax.

AVA. She's probably on her way to a . . . a post office or or . . . a MacDonald's – yeah – some fast food joint where she's gonna, I don't know, burn her bra and shoot till she ain't got any fingers left. Get me out of here, Calvin. Weirdoes stick to me like I'm flypaper. I'm serious.

CALVIN *approaches* KATE. AVA *drops to her knees. Crosses herself every which way.*

AVA. Now I lay me down to sleep . . . oh fuck that's not right. What is it? WHAT IS THE FUCKING PRAYER.

CALVIN puts his hand on KATE's shoulder. She turns to him. A beat. She removes her headphones, puts them in her purse.

KATE. You're from England, aren't you?

CALVIN. I am.

KATE. I knew that.

CALVIN. I'm impressed.

KATE. I was a Pulitzer prize-winning columnist for the Philadelphia Inquirer.

CALVIN. I'm a repossessions man. Depressing, but it's a living.

KATE (*refers to* AVA). Is your friend hurt?

CALVIN. She's praying.

KATE. I like spiritual women.

CALVIN. Do you have a Yellow Pages?

KATE. Yes. I do.

CALVIN. Do you know anything about cars?

KATE. What make?

CALVIN. Chevy Nova. 1974.

KATE. That's the same as mine. What colour?

A beat, before they answer simultaneously.

KATE AND CALVIN. Yellow.

CALVIN. It's my friend's car. Well, I'm in the process of repossessing it, but . . . she's got a night-club engagement she's got to get to in the meantime. (*Refers to the gun.*) Are you afraid of something?

KATE. Everything. (*Refers to his hand on her shoulder.*) You have a very comforting touch.

CALVIN. Thank you. I took a massage class on Long Island.

KATE. New York. You're here from New York?

CALVIN. That's right.

KATE. Is your friend from New York?

CALVIN. Born and bred.

KATE. Really.

CALVIN. I feel I'm meant to marry her. But something tells me she doesn't want it to work out.

KATE. Really.

KATE *gently removes* CALVIN's *hand from her shoulder. She approaches* AVA, *who's been silently praying to herself, eyes shut tight against the threat of potential violence.* KATE *taps* AVA *with the pistol.*

AVA (*with great speed, as if she's been holding this in all the while*). I'm just as uncomfortable with blacks Jews democrats shriners Irish and you know whatever as you are please don't kill me I'm on the verge of a spectacular singing career if only I could find the Tumbleweed Junction.

KATE. I'm a journalist. I don't take sides.

AVA (*she opens her eyes*). Oh. Thankyougod. (*Refers to the gun.*) Is it dangerous around here?

KATE. No. Somebody's watching me, though. What's your name?

AVA. Ava. Ava Coo.

KATE. Ava Coo. Ava Coo. Hmmm.

AVA. Fuck me, not another one who has a thing about my name.

KATE. Are you going out with anybody?

AVA. Oh sure. Maybe. Yeah . . . well. Not really. No. Definitely not.

KATE (*refers to the pistol*). I'll put this away now.

She does. She holds out her hand to AVA. *A beat, before* AVA *takes* KATE's *hand.* KATE *lifts* AVA *to her feet.*

KATE. I understand you have car trouble.

AVA. You ever hear of a club called Tumbleweed Junction?

KATE. Come home with me and we'll discuss it.

Music in: 'Follow Me' (Amanda Lear). Shift to MARTIN and LESTER in an Earls Court gay bar. MARTIN wears his best leathers. LESTER wears his magnificently polished cowboy boots, ten gallon hat, bolo tie: the works. LESTER's not aware he's in a gay bar. He drinks beer and drums his fingers along to the tune. MARTIN watches LESTER take in his surroundings. Several moments pass. MARTIN approaches LESTER. Silence.

LESTER. Man, this place. Wow. Makes me homesick.

MARTIN. Does it?

LESTER. Sure thing. I mean, back home, I got this local place right off the U.S. 220 – called Tinker's. And it's just like this.

MARTIN. Really? How so?

LESTER. Well, it's just about the only place in the entire Shenandoah Valley where a fella can hook up with his buddies, take a break from the missus and the kids. Relax. Shoot some pool. Well. Actually, it's where we have our Klan meetings so, you know, ladies just ain't allowed. (*Beat.*) Still. I didn't think I'd find a place like Tinker's in this neck of the woods. I mean, England's so, I don't know, refined.

MARTIN. We here at the Coleherne take pride in the fact that ladies just aren't allowed. So. Welcome.

LESTER. Why, thank you kindly.

A pause, as they listen to the tune.

LESTER. Great tune, huh? Whatsit, German or something?

MARTIN. Well. It's certainly continental.

LESTER. Yeah. That's what I figured. Sounds like that, that actress.

MARTIN. Dietrich.

LESTER. That's the one. Yeah. (*Beat.*) You look familiar to me. You look like someone I've seen.

MARTIN. I doubt it. (*Beat.*) More lager?

LESTER. That's great, man. I've read that the English peoples have a reputation for hospitality.

MARTIN. I think I've read that, too. (*Produces another lager as if from nowhere.*) Cheers.

LESTER. Yeah. Cheers. (*Beat.*) Calfskin?

MARTIN. Pardon?

LESTER. The chaps. Calfskin, right? The best.

MARTIN. The best.

LESTER. Must have set you back a bundle.

MARTIN. But don't you think it's worth it?

LESTER. You bet. Sure as hell a man's got to be in A-1 shape to wear leather well.

MARTIN. I couldn't agree more.

LESTER. You sure we never met before? In an airport maybe? Strip joint?

MARTIN. I don't travel.

LESTER. Right. Well. (*Beat.*) Is this some kind of biker bar? I mean, everybody's wearing the gear.

MARTIN. We have what you might call theme nights. Sometimes one theme, sometimes another.

LESTER. You a biker?

MARTIN. No. You a cowboy?

LESTER. Coulda been. But, uh, no. I'm in business.

MARTIN. I manage a health club.

LESTER. I'm a politician. Well. I will be. Soon.

MARTIN. Brilliant. You must have great strength. Of character. Do you . . . work out?

LESTER. Who, me? Nah. You got to be kidding.

MARTIN. You look like you work out.

LESTER. Well, you know, in the old days. Boot camp. Infantry. The usual.

MARTIN. I bet you really kicked some ass.

LESTER. Sure. Back then, hell, all the boys kicked a little ass. Now. Well, now I got responsibilities. Got no time for it, buddy.

MARTIN. You ought to make time for it. A fit body is the first step on the road to strength of character.

LESTER. You know, I got to tell you that I truly admire that clean living thing. I do. But . . . there just ain't the hours in a day between the wife, the kid, the, what have you.

MARTIN. The politics.

LESTER. The politics. Damn right. Listen, do you think you could fill me in on the local, you know, the local political scene? The, uh, affiliations and what not?

MARTIN. I don't see why not. Another lager?

LESTER. Gee, thanks an awful lot mister. Don't mind if I do. (MARTIN *produces another lager out of thin air*.) I've been reading about the . . . Tories. That's the ruling party, ain't it?

MARTIN. In a manner of speaking. Yes. The other major parties are Labour and the Liberal Democrats.

LESTER. Well now, we don't like the sound of them Liberal Democrats. Double welfare whammy smells like to me. Which one you belong to?

MARTIN. None of them.

LESTER. So . . . what are you?

MARTIN. You might say I'm a member of a clan.

LESTER. No shit. Who'd a thought . . . well. Ain't that something.

MARTIN. Oh, yes. The American influence is rather strong in my clan.

LESTER (*a brilliant idea occurs to* LESTER). Listen. I'm in the process of teaching my son Ray about, well, just about all sorts of things. History, mainly. Wars. Russia. The important stuff. He's only tiny, you know, three, four months old, but it's crucial to get a head start.

MARTIN. Quite.

LESTER. I was thinking you could tutor him in politics. Me and my wife, we're going to Liverpool for a couple of days. But then we'll be back. And we live, well, just around the corner. So. I mean, if you want to. I'll pay.

MARTIN. I've never been a tutor. But I must say, your proposition is intriguing. (*Beat.*) Do you arm wrestle?

LESTER. Oh now, no shit Sherlock. You're talking to a former Virginia state champeen arm wrestler.

MARTIN. Show me.

LESTER. What? You mean, now? Here?

MARTIN. Show me your arm strength and I'll show you mine.

LESTER (*considers it*). Okay. Sure, you're on. Why not. Flex the old elbow grease.

MARTIN. I like spontaneity in a man. Another sign of character.

They prepare to arm wrestle.

MARTIN. On the count of three.

LESTER. I'm cooking. I'm ready for you, man.

MARTIN (*drawing out the count*). One . . . .two . . . .three.

MARTIN *beats* LESTER *almost immediately.*

MARTIN. Now. Let's talk politics.

Shift to TOM and LORETTA in Greene & Greene pawn shop, Earls Court. TOM works there. LORETTA's browsing. LORETTA carries BABY RAY. The kid's dressed up in LORETTA's ludicrous version of English infant aristocratic chic. So is LORETTA.

LORETTA. Cheerio.

TOM. May I . . . assist you with . . . something?

LORETTA. Tally ho.

TOM. We don't have much jewellery in at the moment, I'm afraid.

LORETTA. Did you know that King Edward the Martyr was killed by his own stepmother in the year of our Lord 978? I think that is absolutely disgusting.

TOM. I don't know. It did happen a long time ago.

LORETTA. Do you suppose he's called a martyr because his stepmother killed him? I mean, would he have been called a martyr had anybody killed him or was it just her? Or is it for some entirely different reason?

TOM. I'm sure I don't know. Can I help you with something in particular?

LORETTA. I am immersing myself in the history and culture of your people. Were you aware that the Romans were olive complected?

TOM. Well. I think, yes, I may have studied that. Once.

LORETTA. Huh. So you knew that? I didn't. Go figure. Are you Mr. Greene?

TOM. No. I'm not. I'm Tom.

LORETTA. Where is Mr. Greene? Or the other Mr. Greene?

TOM. Pardon?

LORETTA. Greene and Greene. Two Greenes. If I'm gonna pawn my double solitaire diamond engagement ring, I'd best be speaking to one of the owners.

TOM. Ah. I'm sorry to disappoint you, but there is just one Mr. Greene. And he doesn't visit the shop very often. He lives in America, you see.

LORETTA. I knew I was attracted to this establishment for a damned good reason. I'm a great patriot. So's my husband. I guess you're in charge, then?

TOM. Yes. I'm the manager. Tom. As I said. Tom Warner.

LORETTA. Oooo. I like that name. Like a movie studio. You're a good looking guy, Tom Warner.

TOM. Why . . . thanks awfully. Really.

LORETTA. I am Loretta, Lady Marquette. And this is my infant son, Baby Ray. Say hello to the nice man, Baby Ray.

LORETTA *waves* RAY's *arm towards* TOM.

LORETTA. Ray's gonna be an Earl or something when he grows up.

TOM. Are you . . . on holiday?

LORETTA. Hell, I ain't worked a day in my life, mister Tom Warner. I am a lady.

TOM. Of course. You did say that. Of course.

LORETTA. Every day's a holiday chez Marquette. I am currently learning several new languages. Shit, every language's a new language these days. So it's best to keep on top of the situation.

TOM. I'm not sure I understand.

LORETTA. Every place you look there's a new country sprouting out the map like some kind of crabgrass. And they all got their own languages. My husband, Lester, he says there ain't no language worth talking but English. But I got this idea, see, that you got to know what your enemies are talking about.

TOM. I hadn't considered that. But you're absolutely, I mean, that's really perceptive.

LORETTA. Damn right. Fact: you go to the UN, there's lots of meetings with these new countries, they're clucking away in their own languages and how do you know they ain't laughing at the U.S.A. behind your back?

TOM. Well. I assume there's simultaneous translation.

LORETTA. You mean those headphone things?

TOM. Mind you, I've not been to the United Nations but I have seen television clips. And . . . as I say, there are translators.

LORETTA. You tell me this, Tom Warner: how do you know those translators ain't laughing at you, too? Huh? Explain that to me.

TOM. I suppose it's a matter of trust. Honour.

LORETTA. Uh-huh. Well. You go on and trust those headphones. You're a very nice young man, I can tell, you've got one eye bigger than the other and that's the surest sign of sincerity in my book. But you are naive, and I do hate to point that out to you.

TOM. I speak a bit of Italian. That's all, I'm afraid. So I probably am naive. I'm sorry.

LORETTA. Now don't go apologising for the state of your human condition, honey. I just been around the block a few more times than you and it's my duty to pass on information. I like you very much, Tom.

TOM. Thank you. Lady Marquette.

LORETTA. You got eyes like my Lester had before he turned mean.

TOM. How many languages do you speak?

LORETTA. Fact: the meaner a man gets, the more his eyeballs shrink. (*Beat.*) I speak a little of this and a little of that. But I'm gonna buy myself some tapes. That's why I'm pawning my engagement ring. Me and Baby Ray, we're gonna listen to a shitload of tapes. How much you reckon you'll give me for the ring, Tom? Tom Warner with the beautiful eyes.

TOM. I'd have to examine it.

LORETTA. Examine away, baby. Last time a man asked to examine something of mine, he found baby Ray nestled up inside me.

LORETTA *gives* TOM *the ring with a flourish. He peers at it through a jeweller's glass.*

LORETTA. I am a student of history. I got to be because my Lester is a very important man and doesn't have the time to study it himself. Like Tammy Wynette says, stand by your man. Course, she also says D-I-V-O-R-C-E spells divorce. But never mind. Listen sugar, what's holding you up? You looking for gold in my double solitaire diamond?

TOM. I'm afraid there's a problem.

LORETTA. Don't frown, Tom. It's not masculine. Open your eyes real big when you talk to me.

TOM. This isn't actually a double solitaire diamond.

LORETTA. You're kidding.

TOM. I'm not an expert, but I do know that this is not what you say it is.

LORETTA. Are you accusing me of lying?

TOM. I didn't say that. I must, however, point out that –

LORETTA. You must nothing. You must hear me when I tell you that I was right there at the Sears Roebuck counter when Lester purchased that ring. I saw the label. It said: DOUBLE SOLITAIRE.

TOM. It's zircon, I'm afraid. Cubic zirconia. Double solitaire.

LORETTA. What are you talking about?

TOM. It's a diamond substitute. It's very convincing, but . . . it's not a diamond.

LORETTA. Are you telling me that my engagement ring is made out of the stuff they sell to housewives who diddle themselves while watching Home Shopping Network?

TOM. I'm not familiar with Home Shopping Network. But I suppose, yes, that is probably what I'm telling you.

LORETTA. Sears Roebuck is a reputable department store.

TOM. Yes, yes. Undoubtedly.

LORETTA. You make much money, Tom?

TOM. I . . . pardon?

LORETTA. Does Mr. Greene or the other Mr. Greene pay you enough money?

TOM. I'm on a fair wage.

LORETTA. Uh-huh. But you ain't rolling in it, right?

TOM. I really can't discuss this with you.

LORETTA. You don't make money. Okay. I won't judge. And I am sure nobody ever sent you to, you know, jewellery expert school, right?

TOM. I have been trained. I have had basic training and Mr. Greene –

LORETTA. You ain't no expert, Tom. Pretty as you are. So I don't think you oughtta be passing judgement on Lady

Marquette's double solitaire engagement ring. That ring is a token of my husband's undying love and devotion to me. It is not a cheap piece of shit.

TOM. I didn't suggest it was. Look. Perhaps another shop will be happy to accommodate you.

TOM *holds out the ring to* LORETTA. *She doesn't take it.*

LORETTA. But I like *you*, Tom. Baby Ray likes you. He's a genius and communicates with me telepathically. What is your sun sign?

TOM. I don't see what it's got to do with anything. (*Beat.*) Taurus. I'm a Taurus.

LORETTA. Baby Ray told me that, you know. A bull, Mommy, that boy with the cock-eyes is a bull, he said. And bulls are strong. But they are often stubborn. You owe me and Baby Ray lunch, Tom.

LORETTA *holds out her hand to* TOM. *She wiggles her fingers impatiently.*

TOM (*rather at a loss, refers to her hand*). Please, Mrs – Lady – Marquette. I can't have fits in the shop. Please.

LORETTA. No, silly. It ain't a fit. Gimme my ring. (*Beat.*) P-U-T the ring on my finger, darlin'.

TOM *slips the ring on* LORETTA'*s finger. It's an awkward movement.*

LORETTA. Ooooo you have made my day, Tom. More years ago than I care to recall, a gorgeous young man like yourself slipped that ring on my finger. He took my breath away. I got asthma now. Well. That was many many stretch marks ago.

TOM. You're not very old now.

LORETTA. Palm reader told me I am the reincarnation of Cleopatra. I got her eyes. Snake eyes. And I got her heavy heavy heart. Take me to lunch.

TOM. Why does your son never make a sound? I mean, babies usually cry or spit or . . . I'm sorry. It's none of my concern.

LORETTA. Baby Ray talks to me the whole time, Tom. You can't hear him is all. See? Just now, he said to me, Mommy, that Taurus man doesn't want to take us to lunch. He doesn't like us, Mommy. Don't you like us, Tom? We're good solid people. You oughtta like us.

TOM. It's not that. Really. But I . . . look, I barely know you and I've got a shop to look after and you have no idea, no idea at all what's been – I mean, it's true that I'm wary of – some of my customers are most unsavoury types you understand – and I don't know what to make of your your – tales of Cleopatra and telepathy and the person I live with despises me 'cos I can't do press-ups but I do try, I really do try to be interested, involved, you know, with his activities and and . . . bloody hell will you please just leave me alone I I I . . . fuck. Shit. I tell him, I do, I say please. Please just leave me. Alone.

A short, sharp cry is heard, presumably from BABY RAY.

TOM. What . . . what was that?

LORETTA. Don't you get a lunch hour, Tom?

TOM. Yes I do. Of course I do. But that's not the – what was that sound? Did your son make that sound?

LORETTA. I'm hungry. So hungry. Feed me.

LORETTA *holds out* BABY RAY *to* TOM. *A pause.*

LORETTA. Well. Come on, boy. Take him. I have an itch I got to scratch.

TOM. I'll drop him.

LORETTA. Ain't you never held a baby, Tom?

TOM. No. Never.

LORETTA. You do it just like you hold a woman. All soft and sure of yourself. I itch real bad, Tom. Take him.

TOM *takes* BABY RAY *from* LORETTA. TOM *holds him as if he's a Martian.* LORETTA *hikes up her skirt and has a long, slow satisfying scratch at her inner thigh.*

LORETTA. Baby Ray doesn't vocalise, Tom. He never speaks out loud. You're just beginning to learn his language.

Shift to AVA *and* TINA. *Music in: 'I Will Always Love You' (Dolly Parton).* AVA's *at* KATE's *house.* TINA's *in her crummy little trailer chopping vegetables, some of them quite inappropriate, for a salad. Far too many vegetables for one salad. During the course of the scene,* TINA's *chopping becomes increasingly frenzied.* AVA *swigs from a bottle of whiskey. Her drinking intensifies as the scene progresses.*

TINA. Mr. Marshall's got this colt called Season's Greetings, you know, on account it was foaled on Christmas Eve? I was right there, knee deep in hay, when it happened. Colt plopped outta its mama and I swear, Ava, I cried. I mean, I do have hay fever so I guess it's no surprise I cried. But I think I was crying about the miracle of birth or the mystery of life or something mystical like I never think about but I should. You know, honey, I was marvelling at this little new-born horsie on Christmas Eve and the words just rolled off my tongue: Season's Greetings, I said to Mr. Marshall. He laughed and wiped some hay off my face and he didn't say nothing, as usual, but later that day I noticed he signed the colt's papers with that lovely name.

AVA. We got a bad connection, Ma. I'm gonna hang up.

TINA. No no honey – don't – don't do that. It's nice hearing your voice.

AVA. It ain't my phone, Ma. And I ain't paying the bill, either. I can't hear a fucking thing you're saying, anyway. Every time I call you I can't hear nothing. Bunch of inbreds built the phone lines in Nevada. I swear.

TINA. What? What's that you said, honey?

AVA. I'm an alcoholic transvestite, Ma.

TINA. That's real nice where you are, Ava. Mr. Marshall's been to Virginia many times because, as you may know, it's an important thoroughbred racing state. Myself, I've never been, but I'd like to. A working woman rarely travels. Tell me all about it. Is the grass really blue?

AVA. How did you – look, I didn't say a thing about Virginia. Not one fucking word. And what are you talking about?

Huh? Kentucky is the bluegrass state, Ma. Not Virginia. I'm dying here. I'm broke and some religious fanatic's come to repossess my car but he won't take the car and he won't leave my side and . . . what in the fuck are you doing over there? Sounds like you got a couple of machetes dancing round your head.

TINA. Your daddy comes from Virginia. 'Course, I don't expect he's there anymore. Not after the murders. Did you get my letter, Ava? Well, it isn't exactly a letter. It's a recording of my voice. It'd be wonderful if you could be here with me. The ranch is so peaceful this time of year. We could eat a salad. I'm eating real healthy. Nothing but vegetables, Ava. Grow em myself. Are you drinking much these days, honey?

AVA. *You're* a fucking vegetable, Ma. LISTEN TO ME.

TINA. Aren't you interested in your daddy? It isn't natural for a girl to lose interest in her father. I lost interest in mine and look where it's got me. Oh, sure, I got myself a fine life with Mr. Marshall but he never talks to me. Sometimes I think if I had kept a healthy interest in my own daddy, I might have noticed I was marrying a man who never speaks. Isn't life funny? Isn't this song pretty? It's my favourite. I listen to it all the time when Mr. Marshall's away. He gave it to me for an anniversary gift.

AVA. God forgive me and I don't know why but I love you Ma. I love you and I don't know where I'm going next and I don't give a shit about some drunk daddy I never met and I sure as fuck don't know how you know where I am but I wish you would just send me some cash and call it a day.

TINA. You still there, Ava? You say something about dinner? Oh honey, I'd love to have you over but Mr. Marshall's bringing a couple of jockeys to the ranch and there just ain't the room for another mouth. Jockeys are funny men. So tiny and polite. You look real pretty today, Ava, that blouse becomes you. But you shouldn't drink whiskey out of a bottle. It isn't lady like.

AVA. I'm going crazy. I'm going crazy and you're scaring me, Ma. I can't take this no more. I only called to fucking say HELLO.

TINA. Hello, honey. Hello. I love saying that word. Hello.

AVA. There's all sorts of things I got to understand. Like . . .
do you really think I can sing? And why do you call the man
you live with Mr. Marshall? Don't he got a name, Ma?
I mean, a name you call him when you're, you know, doing
stuff with him? Private stuff? And why am I on the road to
some nowhere club I can't even locate?

TINA. Hello. Hello. Ava, that word, it thrills me so.

AVA. You ever hear of some place called Tumbleweed
Junction? Huh? Answer *one* of my friggin' questions, Ma,
okay?

TINA. Oh honey, what's the point. Tell me. What is the point
in answering questions when there are so many of them?
That whiskey will rot your gut. My tummy's practically
gone, I've drunk so much whiskey.

AVA. I'm not like you. Don't ever say I'm like you.

TINA. And I wish you wouldn't wear so much black. It's
morbid. Your hair doesn't look healthy. Your skin's so pale.
Let me cook you some soup, honey. Or a stew. Please.

AVA. Look, I gotta go. I gotta . . . this sucks, Ma.

TINA. Hello. Say hello, baby.

AVA. Good-bye, Ma.

Lights down on TINA. *Music out.* AVA *chugs the rest of the
whiskey.* KATE *enters. She holds a casserole dish.*

KATE. I made a stew.

AVA. I used your phone. Long distance. But I don't have any
money, so I can't pay. Tough luck, huh?

KATE. I'm looking for a man.

AVA. Yeah? Well, you can bet he ain't looking for you.

KATE. My phone was disconnected three months ago.

AVA. Uh-uh. No way.

KATE. I don't like talking to people I can't see.

AVA. Well you may not like it, but I just called fucking Las
Vegas.

KATE. Tell me about New York.

AVA. It's big, it's filthy, it's got the World Trade Centre. That about covers it.

KATE. You'll help me find this man I'm looking for.

AVA. Oh no. Nonono. See, me and Calvin are going somewhere.

KATE. You're lost. I found you. Eat some stew.

AVA. I got a job in a club. I'm a night-club entertainer in demand.

KATE. I'm not much of a cook. But I know a few things.

AVA. Hey, lady, you're making my skin crawl.

KATE. I know where your club is. I'm not so bad.

AVA. You what? You know this this . . . Tumbleweed whatchamacalit place? So. Tell me already.

KATE. Scratch my back and I'll scratch yours.

AVA. Oh. Okay. I get it. All right. I'll chow down some of your stew, make a little chit chat, be polite, I tell you you're a great cook, you tell me where the club is. Blah blah blah. I know how to scratch a little back same as the next dope.

KATE. Fine. Then do it.

KATE *sets down the casserole, lifts her shirt, turns her bare back to* AVA.

AVA. Whoa, hold on just a fucking minute. You mean . . . like, you literally want me to scratch your back?

KATE. It's extraordinarily relaxing. I need to be relaxed.

A pause before AVA *begins to tentatively scratch* KATE'*s back.*

AVA. Where's Calvin?

KATE (*really enjoying this*). Ohgodohgodohgod a little higher yes yes no not there a little to the left ohyesyesyes –

AVA. Hey. HEY. I said: where's Calvin?

KATE. Arlington National cemetery. Don'tstopdon'tstopdon't –
theretherethere – ahahahahyessss . . . .

AVA. Aw look, I don't like this shit one bit. Okay?

KATE *pulls away abruptly and pulls down her shirt. After
wallowing in the luxury of the back scratch, she's suddenly
all business.*

KATE. Your turn.

AVA. Thanks, really, but, um, no.

KATE. We have a deal. You scratch my back, I scratch yours.

AVA. Oh man, I'm surrounded by creeps and weirdoes.

AVA, *bored, turns her back to* KATE. *She half-heartedly
lifts up her shirt.*

AVA. I'm all yours. Hurry up.

KATE (*coming up very close to* AVA). I'll take you to
Tumbleweed Junction. I'll drive. You'll sit next to me in the
front seat. You'll wear your seat belt. Calvin will sit in the
back. He doesn't have to wear his seat belt. I'll tell you
stories about this man I'm looking for, you'll tell me about
the Empire State building.

AVA. Sure. Whatever.

KATE. Not whatever. This. This, and only this.

KATE *begins to scratch* AVA's *back slowly, carefully.
Silence.*

AVA. You know, this ain't half bad.

KATE. I told you. It's relaxing.

AVA. My mother's lost her mind. And the really weird thing
is, I don't know if I should give a shit. Oh man, I'm such a
loser. Christ. Look at me. I'm gonna cry. Gotta be PMS.

AVA *angrily wipes at her face.* KATE *gently places her
arms around* AVA's *waist. She rests her head carefully
against* AVA's *bare back. They stand together peacefully,
in silence.*

*Music in: 'Love Is in the Air' (John Paul Young). Lights up
on* OTTO *in* LORETTA *and* LESTER's *hotel room.* OTTO

*carries a gorgeous bunch of flowers. BABY RAY's minia-
ture hooded Klan robe is on the floor. OTTO picks it up,
examines it carefully, finds a ridiculously small portable
telephone in one of its pockets. He drops the robe to the
floor as if it's contaminated.*

*Lights up on CALVIN at Arlington National Cemetery.
John F. Kennedy's grave, with eternal flame. He's on all
fours, crawling around the roped off grave, trying to figure
out how the flame works.*

*Lights up on MARTIN and LESTER regarding a very scary
looking multi-gym. LESTER's never seen one of these
before, and is very much a kid in a candy shop.*

*Lights up on TINA in her trailer, surrounded by mountains
of chopped vegetables. She sits engulfed by them. She eats
salad out of a salad bowl. She watches a tiny portable
television.*

*Lights up on TOM, LORETTA and SUZY in TOM's flat.
They are using an Ouija board, its pointer moving furiously
to and fro beneath their fingertips. BABY RAY is sat on
LORETTA's lap. She's guided his baby-sized fingertips
onto the pointer, as well.*

AVA. My mother listens to songs that nobody else can hear.
I think I'm hearing one of them right now.

KATE. Sssh. I hear it, too.

AVA. Oh yeah? How do you know which one I'm listening to?

OTTO *dials a number on the portable phone.*

OTTO. Reception? Mink here. Yes. Yes. That's right. Three
days, you say? I see. But they haven't checked out. Yes yes
I realise – the clothes on their backs are all they have. Nor
have I seen or heard – that's why I'm here, you fool. How in
the world can you lose track of them for three days?

CALVIN *removes a small pamphlet from his back pocket.
He reads from it.*

CALVIN. The miracle of the eternal flame is, in fact, not so
much a mystery as it is a remarkable feat of engineering and
testament to man's enduring ingenuity. (*A beat as he
considers this.*) Well. Go figure.

LESTER. How long you reckon I got to fiddle with this stuff before there's, you know, an improvement?

MARTIN. You've wasted considerable time, Lester. All of it gone to indolence. Best to begin straight away. On your back.

MARTIN pushes LESTER firmly, but without real force, onto his back on the multi-gym.

LESTER. You know, I'm the kinda guy who just has to think about exercise and a couple of muscles pop out. Look. Here's one in my arm now.

MARTIN looms over LESTER, stands straddling him and the multi-gym.

MARTIN. Been years since you've had a proper workout, though, hasn't it?

TINA (*chomping down salad and watching the telly avidly*). You give it to the fat bastard crook, Oprah honey. You tell him. We ain't gonna take it anymore from scumbags who cut out on their wives. Oh you look just great, Oprah. Trim and tight and lean. I hope you didn't suffer too much for it, honey. I hope you ate lots of salads. I hope that man you're marrying doesn't turn out to be a no account prick. Be careful.

And at TOM's place, the Ouija pointer's jerking about the board at an alarming rate.

SUZY. K-A-T-E-B-U-C-K. Bugger. The bloody thing's spelling out the name of that nutter who's been writing to me.

LORETTA. Hush, woman. Can't you see Baby Ray's concentrating? He's telling us things.

TOM. L-I-V-E . . . .

SUZY. Fuck. I can't take my hand away from the damned thing. Fuck.

LORETTA. Come on, baby. That's a good baby. Tell us things, Ray.

TOM. . . . R-P-O-O-L.

MARTIN (*to* LESTER, *refers to the multi-gym*). Lift your arms, grab hold of the handles and pull down. Push up, pull down. Very simple.

LESTER does so with considerable difficulty. MARTIN lowers himself into a sitting position onto LESTER's lap.

OTTO (*into the phone*). We had a date at the registry office for fuck's sake. Nono – you misunder – Marquette was unaware. Yes yes the divorce papers – look. The woman was to marry me today. Of course she didn't know. Why should she know? It was a bloody SURPRISE, man.

OTTO hurls the telephone down in disgust.

AVA. When's Calvin coming back?

KATE. When the flame dies down.

The Ouija board's pointer movement is at a frenzied peak.

TOM. Liverpool.

LORETTA. G-R-E-E-N-E-M-I-N-K.

SUZY. Greenemink?

LORETTA. Yup. Greenemink.

TOM. Liverpool Greenemink. Huh?

AVA. Hey. What's your name? I don't know your name.

KATE turns AVA around to face her.

KATE. Kate. I'm Kate Buck.

AVA. I'm sorry I used your phone.

KATE. Don't worry. There won't be a bill.

LESTER (*pumping away*). Man, this takes me back to the old days at Fort Bening. And Loretta's really gonna love the new me.

MARTIN quite suddenly grabs LESTER's balls. LESTER starts to let out a scream, MARTIN clamps his hand over LESTER's mouth.

MARTIN. Is she? Well. I don't know when you're going to have the time to show Loretta the new you. You're such a busy boy, aren't you, between your male bonding at Klan meetings and your historical reading. And now, your new fitness regimen. No – don't make a sound. Don't you dare. This is character building, lesson one: take the pain. Oh my: I feel your muscle growing larger as I speak. Transform the pain, Lester. Just close your eyes and think of England. I do.

MARTIN *squeezes* LESTER*'s balls tighter and tighter.*

KATE *leans in towards* AVA, *as if to kiss her.*

The Ouija's pointer begins to spin in uncontrollable circles.

OTTO. LORETTA LORETTA I NEED LORETTA LORETTA I WANT LORETTA WHY LORETTA WHY HAVE YOU BETRAYED ME?

OTTO *drops to his knees and lets out a quite unearthly and long cry of sorrow and deep deep pain. He flings the gorgeous bunch of flowers away. At the moment* OTTO *lets out his cry, these things happen simultaneously:*

KATE, *about to plant a kiss on* AVA*'s lips, covers her ears as if reacting to the most piercing, painful sound she's ever heard.* AVA *faints, dead away.*

MARTIN, *squeezing* LESTER*'s balls ever tighter, hurls himself off* LESTER *and the multi-gym as if he's been hit in the stomach by some mammoth force.* LESTER *hyperventilates.*

TINA*'s tiny portable television set explodes.*

The Ouija board's pointer flies off violently and with great speed, up up and away.

OTTO*'s bunch of flowers lands at JFK's grave at Arlington National Cemetery. The eternal flame is suddenly extinguished.*

And without warning or prelude, the sound of a tremendous approaching storm, like a hurricane or a tornado – wind, like a portent, overwhelms the space. AVA *sits up suddenly, wide awake.*

The space darkens ominously, as if it's closing in on its inhabitants. Everybody looks to the sky as if it holds some kind of common answer.

Blackout.

End of Act One.

Act Two

LESTER *and* MARTIN *in* LESTER*'s hotel room.* LESTER
fidgets with BABY RAY*'s Klan robe.*

LESTER. I know where I seen you before. You're a homo.

MARTIN. Do you think you're telling me something I haven't
  heard before?

LESTER. My wife's up and disappeared on me and I'm stuck
  with a homo fitness freak. (*Refers to the robe.*) This damned
  thing's soaked. Smells salty. Like somebody's been crying
  in it.

LESTER *drops the robe to the floor.*

MARTIN. You've a free will. Go.

LESTER. You're sitting in *my* hotel room, mister.

MARTIN. I was invited.

LESTER. 'Cause I couldn't *move*. I couldn't move an inch
  after what you done to me. You had to help me get back to
  my hotel. You owed me that. Now, I got places to get to and
  I'm running way behind.

MARTIN. Still. I was invited.

LESTER. You live across that air shaft. I seen homos across
  that air shaft. Therefore, you are a homo.

MARTIN. Your analytical skills astound me.

LESTER. Don't look like anybody's home. I seen you there.
  You and your boyfriend.

MARTIN. I knew you had voyeuristic tendencies. Good. We
  can work with that.

LESTER. Dancing around doing, I don't know, weird homo
  shit with weights. I seen it.

MARTIN. Your vocabulary is extremely limited, Lester. There are many more interesting words you could use. For instance: queer, pouf, faggot, nancy boy, ponce. To name a few.

LESTER. I thought you was on the level with me, man. How could you . . . shit. You people disgust me.

MARTIN. You entered my pub. So to speak. You honed right in. Like radar. It's uncanny, wouldn't you say?

LESTER. Hey, man, you caught me off guard.

MARTIN. The refrain of weak men the world over. I could teach you something about overcoming weakness, Lester. If you'd let me.

LESTER. I got no time for you. I gotta find my wife and my son.

MARTIN. She's gone. Done a runner on you, Lester. She smelled the weakness. Same as I do.

LESTER. I shoulda let her go out and catch a flick or something. I shoulda . . . you know, women are way unpredictable.

MARTIN. Moody. Subject to erratic behaviour.

LESTER. Yeah, yeah . . . whoa. I ain't gonna start taking advice from you. You don't know shit about women.

MARTIN. And why not? I probably know more about women than you. Considering how much time you spend at – what was it called? Tinker's?

LESTER. You're a mean motherfucker.

MARTIN. But you like my meanness. Cowards always admire meanness. Though you wouldn't begin to question its source.

LESTER. Hell, I don't got to ask no more questions about you. I already got the answers.

MARTIN. Omnipotence is such an attractive quality.

LESTER. You're talking mumbo jumbo, man, and my watch is ticking.

MARTIN *grabs* LESTER *by his shirt front and pulls*
LESTER *very close to him.*

MARTIN. Listen to me you animal. I come from a place that's
full of light. A light that you have tried to obliterate through
the ravages of scorn and ignorance. Look at me closely,
Lester. LOOK.

LESTER. Don't hurt me, man, don't hurt me or I'll . . . I'll . . .

MARTIN. What? What will you do? Run back to your window
and spy on another couple of queers? LOOK AT ME. What
do you see, tell me. What do you see.

LESTER. Hey, I don't know, you're . . . like, you're a good
looking guy, you're pretty tough and listen, I know you got
lots of friends, okay, I know you got –

MARTIN. Do you see my defences, Lester? I have built an
impenetrable core of darkness to replace all that lost bright
light and believe me, it's wonderful to have you here like
this, up-close and at my mercy.

LESTER. HEY – I AIN'T NEVER DONE NOTHING TO
YOU, MAN. I AIN'T DONE NOTHING.

MARTIN *very suddenly pulls* LESTER *towards him and
kisses him, a deep long kiss. And just as suddenly,* MARTIN
releases him. LESTER *reels backwards.*

LESTER *(frantically trying to wipe the kiss away)*. Oh shit I'm
gonna die now. I'm gonna die I'm gonna die I'm gonna
fucking die –

MARTIN. LOOK AT ME. I'M PERFECT. I'M A
MAGNIFICENT MACHINE. DO I LOOK SICK? I'M
FUCKING IMPERVIOUS.

LESTER *(quite beside himself, tearing at the skin around his
mouth)*. You killed me killed me killed me and now I'm
gonna die I'm gonna die oh sweet Jesus where's my son oh
lord my son my wife my my my –

MARTIN *picks up* BABY RAY*'s robe from the floor.*

MARTIN. You know, Lester, I think the Roman generals
probably snogged each other as a form of greeting. *(Beat.)*
Your tongue is very rough. And salty. Excessive salt intake

is not consistent with the aims of any decent fitness programme. (*Beat.*) Who would have thought we'd see the day when a simple kiss, the purest act of tenderness, could wreak such havoc among the ignorant, and at such cost?

LESTER (*he's babbling*). My son my wife my son my wife my life for yours my life for nothing nothing everything nothing ohohohoh –

MARTIN *helps* LESTER *to his feet. He uses the Klan robe to wipe away the spittle and general mess of* LESTER*'s face.*

MARTIN. I feel the urge to fly. Don't you? I think . . . America. Take me to your leader. Isn't that what you people say when you're captured by the enemy? I do hope you're a good travel companion, Lester.

MARTIN *sneezes three times.*

MARTIN. Must have picked up your bug, eh?

Shift focus to TOM, LORETTA *and* SUZY *in Liverpool.* TOM *holds* BABY RAY *like he's an old hand at infant care. The occasional sound of a train rumbling beneath them.*

LORETTA. This is it. Right here. This is where Baby Ray wants us to be. Liverpool.

SUZY. How do you know?

TOM. She just knows, Suzy. Leave it at that, will you?

LORETTA. Okay. We're here. We're ready. (*Beat.*) What are we ready for?

TOM. Greenemink?

SUZY. There is no such thing as *green* mink. This is foolish. I'm shit scared.

LORETTA. Whatcha scared of, sugar? We're alive and kicking and there ain't a thing can touch us now.

SUZY. How can you be so sure of that?

LORETTA. I believe.

SUZY. In what for fucksake?

LORETTA. In my belief.

TOM. She's got a point, Suzy. I haven't been afraid of
anything since, well, since I've met Lady Marquette.

A particularly loud train passes beneath them.

SUZY. What are we waiting for?

LORETTA. Instructions.

SUZY. From whom?

LORETTA. Who really cares, sweetheart? It's a sunny day and
we got ourselves stood in front of the prettiest building I've
ever seen. Look. Look at the pretty columns, Baby Ray.
They're Roman, I think. Baby Ray's learning lots about the
Romans.

SUZY. This is too weird. It's the eclipse. Got to be the eclipse.

TOM. This is the old law courts, Lady Marquette.

SUZY. Would you *please* stop calling her that? It's driving me
bonkers.

LORETTA. This is the law courts. Fine. Let's go inside and get
us a little justice.

TOM. Brilliant. I've wanted that for such a long time.

SUZY. They're shut down, Tom. *Abandoned.*

LORETTA. Nonsense, woman. I hear them big ole wheels of
justice spinning underneath our feet.

SUZY. Those are trains beneath us, daft bitch.

LORETTA. Suzy the cynical. That figures. But you tell me
this, missy: what's the point of having law courts if they're
closed?

SUZY. How should I know? This is Liverpool. I never question
anything that happens here.

LORETTA. Fact: The wheels of justice never stop spinning,
even if there's nobody home inside the law courts.

TOM. I'd like a hearing before a judge. There's lots I want to
say.

LORETTA. Take my hand, Tom. We're gonna walk together
with our heads held high.

TOM. I'd like that.

TOM *and* LORETTA *join hands.*

SUZY. This is absolutely absurd.

LORETTA. Tell me what kinda justice you're gonna ask the judge for, Tom.

TOM. I . . . there's . . . so much. I mean, there's so much I can't begin to think of what to say.

LORETTA. Okay. I'll start: I want the bastards who make fun of my accent shot through their hearts. Your turn.

TOM. I want . . . a position that matches my qualifications. Yes. That's it.

LORETTA. And Lester will be forgiven for blowing up that truck stop with all them unfortunate people inside.

TOM. Your husband's a murderer?

LORETTA. Well, it wasn't his fault. He didn't know what he was doing. See, we was sitting inside a Chevy Nova with this English fella, you know, he's kinda like Lester's patron or something, and this fella hands Lester something that looks like, whaddyacallit, one of them joysticks? And then he goes, here, Lester, push this button. So Lester pushes the button and boom. Truck stop across the U.S. Highway blows like a geyser. Boom. Just like that, we're fugitives, Lester and me. All cause of some crazy Brit who says Lester's gonna be elected to the U.S. House of Representatives next year and we're all gonna get fat as houses and rich as shit as a result.

TOM. Blimey.

LORETTA. You bet your ass, honey. Okay. So what do we want? One: A better job for my friend with the kind eyes. Two: Me and Lester don't got to be fugitives. What else?

TOM. A satellite dish. A Moroccan holiday.

LORETTA. A set of bone china. An Encyclopaedia Britannica for Baby Ray. And I want . . . titties as sweet and round as melons.

TOM. When I walk into a club, I want people to want me.

SUZY (*reluctantly joining in*). My own astrology column in the Daily Mail. And two dates with Harrison Ford. Okay – one. One f'n date with Harrison Ford.

TOM. To be the most brilliant medical researcher ever. And to snog the bloke with the biggest cock in the world whilst dining with a Royal.

LORETTA. What did you just say, Tom Warner?

TOM. Well. It's justice, isn't it? I'm so happy, Lady Marquette. I can't think why, though.

LORETTA. Baby Ray ain't never been held by no gay.

TOM. Hasn't turned him into a pillar of salt yet, has it?

SUZY. Look. Over there. The doors are opening. The law court is . . . open.

LORETTA. There's the judge.

SUZY. Let's go, Tom. Now. Please.

TOM. She's right. It is a judge. He's bearing gifts.

LORETTA. (*calling out to the unseen presence*). COME ON OVER HERE, MISTER, AND SPREAD A LITTLE OF THAT JUSTICE AROUND.

TOM. I don't believe it. It's Mr. Greene.

LORETTA. No. No it ain't. It's Mr. Mink.

SUZY. Oh no. Greenemink. Minkgreene. It's like that film, you know, Redrum redrum. I'm out of here.

OTTO *enters. He does bear gifts: a letter and some wilted flowers. He smiles an angelic smile. He holds out the letter to* SUZY.

OTTO. Good afternoon, Miss Bradfield. I believe this letter is for you.

SUZY. Who are you? Why have you come out from inside of an abandoned law court? How do you know –

OTTO. Never mind, my dear. You know, the chap who designed these courts committed suicide. A most unfortunate incident. Apparently, his plans called for a rather elaborate inner courtyard, very much like the courtyard which you now face. As luck would have it, our poor architect's fortunes blossomed and he could not supervise the building of these courts. When finally he arrived to witness the opening, he discovered that his inner courtyard had become an outer courtyard. Shortly afterwards, he topped himself. Take the letter, Miss Bradfield. Open it in private.

SUZY *takes the letter.*

LORETTA. That's a truly heartbreaking story, Mr. Mink, but I sure as hell don't why you told it.

OTTO. It's a parable, Loretta.

LORETTA. I don't remember that being in the Bible.

OTTO. Hello, Tom. Have you decided on a bit of a holiday? Did you phone for permission to shut the shop?

SUZY *surreptitiously tries to open the letter.*

OTTO (*without looking at her*). Miss Bradfield. I said: you are to read the contents of that letter in private. (*Beat.*) Well, Tom. What have you to say for yourself?

TOM. I . . . I don't . . . I can't . . . (*Suddenly gains in confidence.*) How is it you're both Mr. Greene and Mr . . . what was it?

LORETTA. Mink. Otto Mink. He's a political media consultant.

OTTO. Sometimes I'm one, sometimes the other. There's no harm in it. And it's really none of your concern.

OTTO *holds out the flowers to* LORETTA.

LORETTA. Gee thanks a bundle. Just what I wanted. Dead daisies.

OTTO. They are not daisies, Loretta. And you could not imagine what I've been through to get them to you. I moved heaven and earth.

LORETTA. Why? What's the big occasion?

TOM. Did you bring something for me, Mr. Greene?

A slight pause, as OTTO *glares at* TOM.

OTTO. Something quite astonishing's about to happen to you, Loretta. Come.

OTTO *holds out his arm to* LORETTA.

LORETTA. Where we going?

OTTO. To the courts, Loretta. The courts.

LORETTA. In there? Is it safe?

OTTO. It's what you want.

LORETTA. Yeah, but, is it *safe*? We gonna get tons of plaster and shit falling on top of our heads? I seen a 911 Emergency episode like that.

OTTO. What do you want? Safety? Or Justice?

LORETTA. You know, they ain't exactly mutually whaddya-callit whatever.

OTTO. Aren't they?

LORETTA. Okay. But I want Tom with me. And Baby Ray. They deserve whatever I end up getting.

OTTO. As you wish. Come, then.

LORETTA *slips her arm through his.*

SUZY. You're not leaving me here, are you?

LORETTA. Find your own justice, sister.

LORETTA, TOM *and* OTTO *begin to exit. The light coming from the direction of the law courts darkens noticeably.*

OTTO. The doors are beginning to close. We must hurry.

LORETTA, TOM *and* OTTO *exit.* SUZY *looks after them as the light grows dimmer and dimmer.*

SUZY. What am I to do? What can I – I've got no *money*. I can't get back. Ooooo FUCK.

SUZY *rips open the letter with some irritation. Several fifty pound notes drop out.*

Lights up on KATE, *behind the wheel of a yellow Chevy Nova. Beside her,* AVA *sleeps, strapped in by her seat belt.*

In the back seat, CALVIN *peers alternately at a map and at the road whizzing by them. They're driving due west.*

CALVIN. What's the town we just passed through?

KATE. Tut's Hut, Idaho.

CALVIN. That's what I thought.

KATE. Why do you ask?

CALVIN. Nothing important, really. It's just . . . it's not on the map.

KATE. I know that.

CALVIN. Oh. All right. (*Beat.*) Why are we speeding? The road's empty.

KATE. You never know what's coming up behind you.

SUZY (*reading from the letter*). Dear Suzy, who needs you. Who. Not me. It's useless to pretend there was no connection between us, nevertheless, who needs you. Not me. Don't pretend you meant to run an ad in a magazine that doesn't exist. I checked it out. Astrology Monthly never existed. Your ad had my name written all over it. But never mind. I have since found my very own personal native New Yorker. We are touring the United States and we are terribly happy together. She doesn't know this yet, but she will in due time. So who needs you. Not me. I am on a mission to find a dangerous terrorist and I feel certain I am getting closer to him. I won't be in touch again because, as you can tell, I am very very VERY busy without you. I'm enclosing one hundred fifty pounds, which, by the way, I had a great deal of difficulty getting in Arlington. But I did get it because I am a decent woman who wants to save you the hassle. The money is not a gift, it's for my chart. If you're such a fucking good astrologer, then you'll have no difficulty guessing my birth details. Good luck. And Suzy, guess what: NOBODY NEEDS YOU LEAST OF ALL ME. Kate Buck.

KATE *slams on the brakes. She blasts the car horn, holds it down.*

CALVIN. What's wrong. WHAT'S WRONG.

KATE *continues to blast the horn;* SUZY *reacts as if she, too, hears the horn wailing away.*

Music in: 'I Don't Know How to Love Him' (Yvonne Elliman). Shift focus to MARTIN *and* LESTER *seated at a table in* MARTIN*'s flat.* MARTIN *eats breakfast and reads a tabloid. He's enjoying the music.* LESTER *isn't eating. He just stares at* MARTIN. *This goes on for some time.* MARTIN *sneezes once.*

MARTIN. Eat something.

LESTER. I'm on a hunger strike. All political martyrs do hunger strikes.

MARTIN. Suit yourself.

More silence from LESTER; MARTIN *continues with breakfast, music and tabloid.*

LESTER. You're holding me hostage.

MARTIN. Here's a sordid little story. Bloke in America plants a bomb in a truck stop. Kills twenty-seven Baptist ministers.

MARTIN *sneezes twice.*

LESTER. Kidnapping is a federal offence, buddy.

MARTIN. So is murder. Why do you suppose twenty-seven Baptist ministers convened at a truck stop?

LESTER. I could send you down on lots of charges. This ain't legal.

MARTIN. Are you able to walk, Lester?

LESTER. Yeah, yeah. I can walk. What's it to you?

MARTIN. Then walk. Leave. I don't see that you're shackled or bound and gagged. Would you like to be bound and gagged?

A pause, as LESTER *considers this.*

LESTER. Maybe them Baptist preachers had it coming to them.

MARTIN. Why do you stay, Lester? Why did you follow me back to my flat? What's the fascination? (*Mocking* LESTER, *sings along to the song.*) I don't know how to love him . . . what to do . . . how to moooove him.

MARTIN *coughs a bit.*

LESTER. Maybe them Baptist preachers was spies. Or traitors.

MARTIN. For whom were they spying?

LESTER. You know, whoever . . . spies *spy* for. Other governments. Enemies.

MARTIN. Well, I'm sure they gathered loads of valuable information in Denny's Roadside Diner. (*Beat.*) The murderer will surely get the gas chamber, don't you think?

LESTER. Yeah, well, he's a hero in my book. I mean, just twenty-seven less nigger preachers to deal with. Hardly a dent in the, you know, the iceberg.

MARTIN. The story does not refer to race one way or the other.

LESTER. Sure, but, deep south, it stands to reason Baptists are . . . shit man, in Virginia every other Baptist's a nigger snake handler.

MARTIN. I didn't say where the truck stop was. In fact, it *was* in Virginia. Lynchburg, Virginia. How appropriate. And how perceptive of you.

LESTER. I'm pretty fucking smart, mister. (*Beat.*) You been listening to this pussy song all morning. I'm gonna vomit all over your pristine faggot floors, you don't turn it off.

MARTIN *coughs a bit more.*

MARTIN. What's wrong, Lester, did you sleep through the seventies?

LESTER. You think I'm stupid, right? I'm not stupid. I know this song. I know it comes from some fucked up Limey musical thee-a-ter thingamajig with a bunch of hippies humping Jesus and and . . . sacrilegious crap, that's what it is. People will buy any old shit but not me. No sir. I know what's what.

MARTIN. This from a man who applauds the murder of twenty-seven black Baptist ministers. Let me ponder that one. You're obviously way ahead of me.

LESTER *overturns the table. Music out.* MARTIN *has a violent sneezing and coughing fit. A pause, as neither man moves.* SUZY *enters, carrying a tabloid. She looks very much worse for wear.*

SUZY (*excitedly, referring to the tabloid*). She really is looking for a man. A terrorist. Christ. She actually is a journalist. Here. HERE. Kate Buck. Kate Buck. This story is fantastic. Absolutely brilliant. A dangerous felon on the lam and Kate Buck pursues his trail against the odds. Brilliant. (*Notices, for the first time, the overturned table, etc.*) Have I interrupted something important?

A pause. The men ignore her. They are absolutely focused on one another, neither moving the tiniest bit. SUZY *isn't clocking anything, though, and sets about cleaning up the mess, re-righting the table and such.*

SUZY. Anyway, isn't it funny how things turn out? Here I was thinking she was a first rate nutter with an alias. I mean, I hadn't any reason to think she was *actually* called Kate Buck. It's got a sort of Mills and Boon ring to it, you know? I'm impressed. Really. She's risking her all for . . . for . . . well, I don't know exactly *why* she's doing it, God knows I wouldn't, but I'm sure it's for the best.

MARTIN (*without losing his focus on* LESTER). Where've you been, Suzy?

SUZY. You look awful, Martin.

MARTIN. Bit of the flu.

SUZY. Ah. (*Beat.*) I think she's really admirable. In context. She wants me to do her chart.

MARTIN. Where've you been, Suzy?

SUZY. Liverpool. (*Beat.*) Honestly, Martin, have I interrupted . . . you know . . . (*Takes notice of* LESTER.) Oh. Hello. How rude of me not to have introduced myself. Suzy Bradfield. Astrologer.

She offers her hand to LESTER. *He doesn't take it.*

LESTER. I got to go to Liverpool.

SUZY. Oh. Holiday?

LESTER. Business. Big business.

MARTIN. Where's Tom?

SUZY. Tom. Well. Tom's been kidnapped.

MARTIN. He isn't worth the trouble.

SUZY. It's not really . . . look, I suppose he hasn't been kidnapped. But he has gone away. With a woman.

LESTER. *I've* been kidnapped.

SUZY. How horrible for you. Was it terribly frightening?

LESTER. I am Martin's hostage. Right now.

A pause, as SUZY *considers this. The men have kept their focus on each other.*

SUZY. Ah. Yes. Well, I'm sure you'll work it out between yourselves.

MARTIN. So. Tom's done a runner with a woman.

SUZY. And her child.

MARTIN. Oh. A tot, as well. Fucking brilliant. Who's going to do the washing up now?

A pause, as MARTIN *smiles maliciously at* LESTER.

LESTER. I got to get to Liverpool. I got a job to do. I got to find my wife.

SUZY. Well, I suggest you catch a train from Euston. They run fairly regularly and it's not a bad journey, not really, considering . . . I'm sorry, I didn't catch your name . . .

LESTER. Lester Marquette. Political candidate for election to the U.S. House of Representatives, state of Virginia.

SUZY (*after a beat*). Fucking hell. You're . . . no. It can't be. A coincidence, a really strange coincidence. Have you noticed the alarming rate of coincidences lately? Kate Buck says –

LESTER. What coincidence? Why are you looking at me that way, lady? Huh? Whatcha looking at?

SUZY. The terrorist. In Kate Buck's story. He's called Lester Marquette, too. Isn't that weird? You know, I feel I know Kate Buck so well.

MARTIN *laughs.* LESTER *snatches the tabloid from* SUZY *and scans it frantically.* MARTIN *continues to laugh.*

LESTER. Oh shit. Oooooh shit. Man, I got to get in touch with Mink. Where the *fuck* is he? WHERE? No names. Supposed to be no names mentioned. NO NAMES. NO GOD-DAMNED NAMES.

MARTIN's *laughter is now mixed with coughs and sneezes.* LESTER *slumps back, unable to cope with this new information.* SUZY, *at a complete loss, continues to clean.*

SUZY (*to* LESTER). Ehm. I hope you don't mind me asking, but, are you really a member of the Ku Klux Klan?

A pause, as LESTER *regards* MARTIN *coolly.* MARTIN's *coughing/laughing seizure is now really alarming.*

LESTER (*to* SUZY). You got any cough syrup, lady?

Shift focus to TINA, *on the job in the ladies room at Tumbleweed Junction. She scrubs at the floor with a pathetic, basically eaten away foam sponge. She occasionally dips the sponge into a bucket of dirty water. Distant sounds from the casino: slot machines, bells, sirens.* TINA *speaks into the miniature Dictaphone.*

TINA. Dear Ava. As I can't seem to remember the details of our last telephone conversation, I thought I'd send along another tape. It's weird that I can't remember what we spoke about. There was an eighty-eight-year-old woman on Phil Donahue's show who woke up one morning unable to remember anything that happened to her after her tenth birthday party. A psychiatrist said she'd been traumatised. And I thought, well, why did the trauma wait eighty years to hit? Seems like everybody's traumatised these days and really, Ava, I am ashamed to say I do not buy it. But who am I? I'm not an expert, so maybe that's what happened to us. Trauma, which was carried by the telephone line. Like lightning, which I have heard does strike people through telephone lines more frequently than you might imagine. Ava, I will be honest. Things are not good and I'm not sure I have the strength to continue at Tumbleweed Junction. There hasn't been any toilet paper here going on two weeks and Mr. Greene hasn't turned up in days. I don't got any

cleaning materials, and the toilets are in an awful mess.
I mean, I tried to use some lye soap I kept for emergencies
in the trailer, but that ran out pretty quick. I guess casino
gambling gives people the runs. I didn't get my last pay
cheque and God knows when Mr. Marshall's gonna show up
and really honey, I don't think he's gonna turn up at all but
I got to believe he will. So most days I show up at the casino
out of habit and I scrub the floor with water, but it's no
good. No good at all. It's like my routine has become a
memory of its former self but since the memory ain't a fond
one, what's the point? Oh Ava, I fear I'm not making a
damned bit of sense.

Lights up on CALVIN *and* AVA. AVA *sorts through an
open suitcase full of outfits for her club routines. She hands
one to* CALVIN.

AVA. Whaddya think?

CALVIN. It's very . . . Shirley Bassey.

AVA. You think?

CALVIN. Yes, yes I do. It's not a bad way to go, Ava. Gold-
    finger is a night-club classic.

AVA. Nah. It's too, you know, too queeny.

CALVIN. But you're a female impersonator, Ava. There is a
    certain logic to doing something queeny.

AVA. Yeah, but . . . I wanna do something, I don't know,
    daring. Not expected.

CALVIN. How about Joan Baez? I've always liked Joan Baez.
    She's politically aware and I admire that in popular singers.

AVA. Uh-huh. Well, I do Joan Baez and I'll bore the audience
    to death. All that Gracias a la whatever shit.

CALVIN (*clearly a bit hurt*). I'm sorry. It was just a
    suggestion.

TINA. I been thinking about your daddy so much, Ava. I don't
    know why. And that was before I seen that newspaper story
    about his latest criminal activities. It's amazing how you can
    go for years without thinking of somebody and then . . .
    well, there may be a reason for everything, but I can't figure

out a reason for anything. I think that's why we have
philosophers, to figure out those reasons. But I have noticed
that most philosophers tend to be French or German, and not
American, I guess 'cause in those countries way back when,
there was nothing to do but think. Americans were busy
building roads and putting the Injuns in their place and
dealing with, you know, all the stuff we had to catch up with
on account of us being a new country. So if we don't got
philosophers here, I wonder if that means we are doomed
never to think of the right answers for why stuff happens.

AVA. Listen, Calvin. I like you. But you ain't the king of style,
I gotta say. (*Beat.*) So what's she doing in there, palm
readings or mind readings or whatever that scary stuff she
does is? I swear, I wish the ground woulda swallowed me up
back there in that, that . . . what was that loony tunes place
we was at yesterday?

CALVIN. Brighton Village. A reproduction early American
settlement.

AVA. Yeah, like Disneyland except instead of Mickey Mouse
you got fucking Puritans or something and half naked yo-
yos painted red to look like Indians except it's so hot the
makeup blisters all over their bodies and they end up
looking like goddamned lepers and wacko Kate tells one of
them he would end up in the fucking slammer before
Christmas on grand theft auto charges and I coulda died, I
coulda just died of embarrassment right there in front of the
imitation ye oldee worldee Martha Washington.

CALVIN (*after a beat*). Kate is not a wacko.

AVA. No. Not exactly. She's more like a wackette.

CALVIN. She cares for you a great deal. Why do you never
notice when people care for you, Ava?

AVA (*after a beat*). Okay. She's not so bad. Okay?

CALVIN. And you should have paid more attention to
Brighton Village. It's a remarkable piece of living history.
Especially the silversmith's –

AVA (*extremely irritated with him*). Why don't you just blow it
out your ass already?

TINA. I know I said it before but I got to say it again and again
    so it makes sense to me: things are not good. They are not
    good at all, Ava. I'm too old to be on my knees all day and I
    don't like the way the hotel customers sneer at me on their
    way to the john, like they're saying, hell, that hag's too old
    to be scrubbing floors even though I ain't old at all, honey,
    hell, I'm barely past forty I think. It's just I look older than
    time itself and yes, maybe that's because I had one husband
    who fucked off when I gave birth to a girl and now I got
    another one who can't stand me so much he lives in his
    truck. But I can't help thinking it's also got something to do
    with the fact that I got a daughter who ain't interested in
    where she comes from anymore. Those casino gamblers
    look at me while they're pissing out champagne and I hear
    them thinking. They think: why have the toilet scrubber's
    children let her get to that state? It's criminal. And I got to
    admit, Ava, I got to ask: don't you feel ashamed, honey?

CALVIN. Kate's filing her new story. Information comes to
    her in dreams, in odd flashes of deduction while she's
    driving. She says it's like a thousand piece jigsaw puzzle of
    a Jackson Pollock painting. Unfathomable but logical. And
    you've inspired that. I envy her.

AVA. I wouldn't spend too much time envying Kate I'm-
    Dreaming-As-Fast-As-I-Can Buck. Didn't she get fired from
    her last job for dreaming up information?

CALVIN. That was a different situation, at a different time.

AVA. Facts are facts. Where I come from, newspaper types
    deal in facts, not in the twilight zone.

CALVIN. Fact is relative sometimes.

AVA. Uh-huh. Well, my mother's a relative sometimes.

TINA. I got fifteen dollars and thirty-nine cents in my checking
    account and Mr. Marshall's absconded with the two hundred
    dollars in my Christmas Club account. So there's no gifts in
    your future this year, Ava. There's no gifts in mine, either.
    My t.v. blew up the other day and the trailer shook right off
    its foundation. And I don't know why I'm recording this
    stuff honey, because you and me both know I'm never
    gonna send you the tape. The truth ain't never been a help to

neither one of us but oh God I sure wish I knew what could be a help to us 'cause we need it bad.

TINA *drops the Dictaphone into the bucket of dirty water.*

AVA (*clutches at her chest*). Christ. Feels like my lungs are filling up with water. Shit. I think I'm *drowning*.

CALVIN *moves to help her.*

TINA. Hell with it. I'm going for broke at the slots.

TINA *tosses the sponge into the bucket of dirty water. She begins to exit, turns back, retrieves the Dictaphone from the bucket and exits.*

CALVIN. Stress. Too much stress in one so young. You should read more often. Reading relaxes as well as informs.

AVA. Get your hands off me. (*He does.*) You got cold hands, Calvin, and books give me a headache. (*A beat.*) Phew. I feel much better now.

AVA *rummages through the suitcase, picks out an outfit.*

AVA. Rosemary Clooney. That's original. Whaddya think?

Shift focus to TOM, LORETTA *and* BABY RAY *in the Liverpool law courts.* LORETTA *breast feeds* BABY RAY. *They wander around in circles.*

LORETTA. Looky there. They got the stations of the cross up on the wall.

TOM. I don't think so. It's not a church.

LORETTA. Honey, church, court – same thing back where I come from. Oh my, and they're three dimensional stations, too. Look: you can see Jesus' blood trickling down from his crown of thorns.

TOM. I don't know how long we've been here. I've lost track of time.

LORETTA. Coupla days, I reckon. Or maybe a week. Who knows? Mr. Mink/Greene said we'd be provided for and I believe him. Ooooo look at Saint Veronica making a photocopy of Jesus' face with her handkerchief.

TOM. Do you miss your husband, Lady Marquette?

LORETTA. You know, I don't. I expect he's doing okay for himself. Lester's kind of a weasel and I spend a lot of time convincing him he's smart when really he's got the IQ of a flea, but I like the way his hair stands on end in the morning like it's full of electricity.

TOM. But what's it like waking up next to a criminal?

LORETTA. Lester's not a criminal, sweetheart, he just wants to be famous. Don't you want to be famous?

TOM. Not really.

LORETTA. That's a true shame, Tom Warner.

TOM. Why?

LORETTA. I don't know. It's just something solid to believe in, like when you call the talking clock and it tells you the exact time.

TOM. I've always wanted to own my own beauty salon, but it's a bit of a gay cliché, so . . . But I do like hair. Not to cut it, mind you, but to wash it, run my fingers through a really smashing head of hair, you know?

LORETTA. Lester's going bald.

TOM. I never feel close to a man until I run my fingers through his hair. I'd be able to do that all day long in my own beauty salon and never have to put up with the rest.

LORETTA. The rest of what?

TOM. You know, the whole lot. Dating, clubbing, sex, possible commitment, more sex, more dating, too many clubs, bad performance art, disillusionment, less sex, no sex, the end.

LORETTA. Hell, that sounds just like real dating between men and women, except for the performance whatever. You got such pretty eyes, Tom. I bet you could have any sailor in port.

TOM. My flatmate makes me feel inadequate. (*Beat.*) Sailors are a bit passé, Lady Marquette.

LORETTA. I am trying to make some social chit-chat around a difficult subject, okay? Don't make it harder on me.

TOM. Don't you think it's strange that we've been here for rather a long time without getting hungry?

LORETTA. Nope. I figure it's a test.

TOM. What sort of test?

LORETTA. A really hard one. (*Beat.*) Sailors in Roanoke are mighty handsome. Strong. Lean. Great heads of hair. God, I miss home. I mean, I like this submersion in alternative cultures just fine, but I hate being on the run and I'm a real mountain girl at heart.

TOM. The Blue Ridge Mountains. (*Beat.*) I was always good at geography.

LORETTA. That means you got a wandering soul.

TOM. Say – if Roanoke is basically a valley surrounded by mountains, why are sailors stationed there?

LORETTA. Beats me. Just another military mystery, I guess.

TOM. And most sailors I know are a bit short and pallid. Why are they so hunky in Roanoke?

LORETTA. Well, probably 'cause they don't get to do naval duties much on account of the lack of water so they spend all their time in gyms or something.

TOM. Sounds like paradise.

LORETTA. Tom. Let's go. You and me and Baby Ray. Let's go home. To Roanoke.

TOM. It's . . . very tempting. But I couldn't.

LORETTA. Why the hell not? You tell me what's keeping you here.

TOM. Things. My job. Things.

LORETTA. There's no gay running a beauty salon in Roanoke, Tom. Believe me. You'd be the first. Hell, it'd be kinda like a monopoly.

TOM. Well. I do love the idea of a monopoly.

The sound of a massive set of doors opening, straining, as if they've been shut for a thousand years. A brilliant shaft of golden light streams across TOM.

LORETTA. Praise be something or other, Tom. Them doors are opening. And look at you, all bathed in sunlight.

TOM. The light. It's so warm. Gloriously warm. Why are the doors opening now?

LORETTA. We found justice, that's why. Come on. We're going home.

Shift focus to SUZY *and* LESTER *in* MARTIN's *flat.* SUZY *is reading* LESTER's *palm.*

LESTER. Can you see where my wife's at?

SUZY. It doesn't work that way.

LESTER. Does it say something about my son?

SUZY. I'm afraid it doesn't *say* anything. Palms don't talk.

LESTER. Yeah, but them lines talk. That's what you said.

SUZY. Well, yes, metaphorically speaking, the lines . . . speak.

LESTER. Well, then what's the problem, woman? Are my lines mutes?

SUZY. No. It's . . . look. Lately, Mr. Marquette, I seem to have been blessed with the power of second sight. I mean, I know that because I am an astrologer, people assume I have special gifts in all things paranormal. But let's be frank, we both know that all most astrologers do is buy a software programme, run a few dates through a PC, and end up with a twenty-page printout of platitudes for which some poor sod is out of pocket thirty quid. And that is exactly what I did until a fortnight ago. Now, I know when road accidents are about to happen, I know when certain people will develop pancreatic cancer, I know the eclipse has a huge role to play in my future, and I am now obsessed with a woman I had written off as a lesbian psychopath a mere fourteen days ago. So excuse me if I encounter a few problems in reading your palm.

LESTER. I can't leave Martin. I hate him, but every time I get up to walk out that door, I think, hey, man, you gotta do a few more dishes or there's dust under the couch I got to clean up.

SUZY. He has that effect on people.

LESTER. I wanna strangle him and kind of like, you know, hang out with him. All at the same time. Used to be, a guy could rely on another guy. Hell, he could rely on *any* other guy, even a foreign guy, to share a similar viewpoint on most things. Like it was some big club where all the rituals was secret and yet every guy knew them. Now, well, who knows, you know?

SUZY. Yeah. I know. (*A beat, as she scrutinises his palm.*) I'm seeing . . . jewellery.

LESTER. Jewellery?

SUZY. Yes. And . . . guitars. Electric guitars. Toasters. Bric-a-brac. How very odd.

OTTO MINK *appears, as if from nowhere.*

OTTO. Hello, Lester. You're looking remarkably shitty.

LESTER. Fuck. I mean, Mr. Mink – when – where – I mean –

SUZY (*to* LESTER, *refers to* OTTO). You know this bloke?

LESTER. Damn right. He's my my whaddycallit my . . .

OTTO. Brains? (*Beat.*) Lovely to see you again, Miss Bradfield. Tell me, was that letter informative?

SUZY. I see bad things. Very bad things.

OTTO. Pessimist. (*To* LESTER.) I've got some good news and some bad news, old chap. The bad news is: there's been a change in plan. I will no longer be requiring your services in the U.S. House of Representatives. The good news is: I've a new job for you and you won't have far to go to get it. Henceforth, you will refer to me as Mr. Murphy Greene.

LESTER. What the hell's going on here, Mink? You made promises. You made a lot of promises.

OTTO. I promised you a job. That is all.

LESTER. Yeah, but –

OTTO. But nothing, Lester. (*He produces a sheet of paper out of thin air.*) I own a pawn shop. The shop is not far from here. The address of the shop is written down on this sheet of paper. You will take this sheet of paper and you will go to the shop.

SUZY. Toasters. Guitars. Jewellery.

LESTER. Hey, I ain't no fucking cheap shop clerk.

SUZY. Bric-a-brac. Pancreatic cancer. Kate Buck.

OTTO. No, Lester. But you will be a fucking cheap shop assistant. And soon.

SUZY. Fifteen car pile-up on the M4. Jack-knifed semi. Bric-a-brac. Kate Buck. Kate Buck.

OTTO. I believe Miss Bradfield's really rather lost it.

OTTO dangles the sheet of paper and the key for LESTER. A beat. LESTER, defeated, approaches OTTO to accept them.

Music in: 'Mesopotamia' (The B52s). Insistent sounds of casino gambling in full swing. Shift focus to KATE, AVA and CALVIN. They have arrived in Las Vegas and are admiring the formidable facade of the Luxor Hotel. KATE reclines against a telephone box which has been made up to resemble an Egyptian sarcophagus. CALVIN furiously snaps photos of the pyramid and Sphinx. AVA wears a beaded gown – possibly her Shirley Bassey outfit. She chugs a Budweiser tall boy.

CALVIN (*to no one in particular, as he snaps away*). The Sphinx. From Greek myth, an inscrutable beast with the body of a lion and the head of a woman, who killed travellers when they could not provide answers to the riddles she asked them.

AVA. Oh yeah? In that case, I got lots of riddles I'd like to ask lots of people. (*To KATE, referring to the phone box.*) What's up with you and that coffin, huh? It ain't exactly gonna fly away without you.

KATE. Aren't you a little overdressed?

AVA. This is Vegas. There's no clocks and no dress code.

KATE. I'm expecting a call.

AVA. Look. We been standing here three hours. I'm getting varicose veins.

KATE. If there's no clocks, how do you know we've been here three hours? (*Beat.*) I'm very close to him, Ava. I'm on my way.

AVA. Oh, you know, I've had it up to here with being on *your* way. I wanna *arrive*, all right?

KATE. By the way, Calvin, the Sphinx killed herself when Oedipus answered one of her supposedly unsolvable riddles. So much for inscrutability.

CALVIN (*pretty miffed*). I knew that. I did. I just chose not to include it in my retelling. You can be such a bad sport, Kate.

AVA. Knock-Knock: who's there? Ava. Ava who? Ava I WANNA FUCKING ARRIVE ALREADY.

KATE. What's got two heads, a beer belly, a nasty disposition and yet is somehow entirely loveable?

AVA. I don't know. What?

Lights up on OTTO. *Music out. The telephone rings. A pause, as* KATE, AVA *and* CALVIN *regard the ringing sarcophagus.* KATE *jumps to answer it.* CALVIN *and* AVA *are all ears.*

OTTO. It's been too long since last we spoke, Miss Buck.

KATE. I'm close. Tell me I'm close.

OTTO. Still listening to sentimental popular music, eh? Well, I must admit the events of the last two weeks have brought me somewhat closer to your point of view. (*Beat.*) Yes. You are close, Miss Buck.

KATE. I knew it I knew it I smell his blood I KNEW it. Where do I go now?

OTTO. Tell me, why are you so anxious to pursue this individual now that you've found love? You have found love, haven't you, Miss Buck?

KATE. Yes. I have. Or . . . as close as I can get. But that doesn't mean I can't have both.

OTTO. You will catch the next flight to London. You will proceed to a certain pawn shop, Greene and Greene, in Earls Court.

KATE. Yes, but what about . . . (*Keenly aware that* AVA *and* CALVIN *are listening.*) well, the matter we just discussed?

OTTO. I have no answer, Miss Buck, except to suggest that the choice is more clear cut than you imagine. I speak sentimentally. From experience.

KATE. She . . . the matter we discussed is my sole inspiration. I can't leave her behind.

OTTO. I am a businessman, Miss Buck. Inspiration is cheap. American Airlines, flight 666, three o'clock. Be on it.

KATE. Nono – wait – there's no clocks in Las Vegas. I can't tell time. I CAN'T TELL TIME.

Lights down on OTTO. KATE *hangs up, remains inside the telephone box.*

AVA. You gonna tell me where this club is now? Come ON. Chop chop.

KATE. Do you believe in fate, Ava?

AVA. Fuck that. I got a gig.

KATE. Tumbleweed Junction's right behind you.

AVA. What? You mean, naaah. It's too big. It's too . . . something.

CALVIN. No, Kate. This isn't Tumbleweed Junction. It's the Luxor Hotel, the ninth wonder of the world.

KATE *exits the phone box, approaches* AVA.

KATE. You look magnificent in that gown, Ava Coo.

AVA. Jeez, hey, I don't need . . . thanks. Really. I appreciate, you know, whatever.

KATE *takes* AVA *into her arms and kisses her, a long, gentle, sensual kiss.* CALVIN, *at a bit of a loss, snaps photos of their kiss.* KATE *releases* AVA, *takes* AVA'S *Budweiser tallboy, and exits. A considerable pause, as they consider her leave-taking.*

AVA. Hey. She never did say what had two heads and a beer belly.

Sudden intensification of the casino gambling sounds. AVA and CALVIN turn to face the Luxor Hotel. They walk towards its entrance.

Shift focus to OTTO and TINA in TINA's trailer. TINA eats a bowl of salad and stares at her burnt out portable television set. OTTO regards his waterlogged Dictaphone.

OTTO. Tell me about love, Mrs. Marshall.

TINA. Are you a philosopher?

OTTO. I chose against it many years ago.

TINA. I'm sorry about the Dictaphone. I got a little, well, over excited.

OTTO. Have you heard from Mr. Marshall?

TINA. Yeah, sure. Maybe. Well, no. But I heard from my daughter. That's something.

OTTO. Do you believe there is such a thing as a broken heart?

TINA. I think . . . I've got to be able to see something in order to know that it's broken. My t.v.'s busted. I know that.

OTTO. Therefore, if one has left behind the object of one's desire, if the love one harbours is no longer in sight, one doesn't really know if the love is destroyed.

TINA. Yeah, I guess that's right. And since I haven't *seen* Mr. Marshall in a dog's age, I got nothing to worry about. (*Beat.*) Are you French or German by any chance, Mr. Greene?

OTTO removes his wallet from his jacket pocket and sets it down beside TINA.

OTTO. For your television set. Thank you, Mrs. Marshall. (*Beat.*) Is the salad tasty?

TINA. Mmmm. Fresh veggies. Grow 'em myself. You want some?

OTTO. There's a perpetual order on loo paper and cleaning supplies at Tumbleweed Junction. I shan't be returning.

TINA (*peeks inside the wallet*). Mr. Greene, this is way too much money for a t.v. repairman and really you don't got to –

OTTO (*patting his hand over hers, an affectionate touch*). Sssh. Are those cherry tomatoes?

TINA. Oh, sure. They're real easy to grow.

OTTO. I'm suddenly quite famished.

TINA feeds OTTO salad out of her bowl. She uses her fork. He eats greedily, gratefully.

Shift focus to MARTIN, who stands before a full length mirror. He wears only briefs and a peaked leather cap. He coughs. He's shivering, sweaty, sniffly, sneezy. He's very sick. He strikes various poses, à la Mr. Universe.

MARTIN. Steel steel steel steel steel steel steel steel steel rock rock rock rock rock rock hard hard hard hard hard hard march march march march forward forward forward back back back forward back forward back west west west west Calvin Calvin Calvin Calvin . . .

OTTO enters.

OTTO. Are you ready, Martin?

MARTIN. Ready ready west ready west ready fly fly fly fly fly up up down up down up up down down fly fly fly fly west west west west . . .

Shift focus to AVA. She stands at a microphone, ready for her big act. She wears a rather strange outfit and a ridiculous blonde wig. She looks like nobody in particular. She holds an electric guitar. She taps the microphone a couple of times and gets feedback.

AVA. Shit. Whoops. I mean, hey, it's really great, really outstanding to be with y'all here tonight. It's taken me a while to get here and lemme tell you, I learned more than I ever wanted to know about the Revolutionary War, the Amish, and other assorted religious types who don't have sex. But I'm with you now, and that's the important thing.

Lights up on TINA and CALVIN playing the slots side by side at the Luxor. TINA hits a small jackpot.

CALVIN. You're very lucky.

TINA. Somebody gave me a bunch of money today. I have this theory about money coming to money. So I'm investing all the cash I got in the slots.

CALVIN. Gambling isn't an investment.

TINA. Says who?

AVA. I'm gonna sing a special tune for you tonight. It's for this friend of mine, see, who kinda took off sudden, you know, without advance warning. I hate when that happens, don't you?

CALVIN. I've lost ten dollars.

TINA. That's nothing, son. A drop in the bucket. I know all about buckets. Use 'em a lot in my line of work.

CALVIN. You remind me of somebody.

TINA. Well I sure hope it's Zsa Zsa Gabor.

AVA. I thought I hated her a lot but then she scratched my back and I felt, I don't know, a connection, a safety, and it was confusing to me because I thought I hated her and . . . well, I mean, it wasn't sexual or nothing 'cause, shit, what do I know about sex anyway? I'm just some chick who pretends to be a chick so people will look at me in a different light so, Christ, you know, what's *that* about?

CALVIN. I was interested in the socio-political implications of gambling in the late twentieth century.

TINA. And now you're not interested?

CALVIN. I put a quarter in the slot and suddenly I no longer cared about the implications.

AVA. Anyways, this is for my friend who I didn't think I liked at all but then she scratched my back and later on she kissed me and though it was nothing sexual it was something sexual and fuck knows I don't understand it at all and all I really know is I miss her now she's gone and I ask you, ain't that always the way?

CALVIN. My friend's performing in the Euphrates Lounge. She's a female impersonator. She's quite good.

TINA. Does she do Dolly Parton?

CALVIN. Uhm, no. I don't think she does. But she does others. Many others.

TINA. No, honey, I'm not interested. I have no time for unknown quantities.

AVA. Okay. So. Here it is. My song for you.

Music in: 'Bette Davis Eyes' (Kim Carnes). AVA begins her lip synch routine. For some reason, she's amazingly convincing. CALVIN and TINA continue on at the slots. AVA grows in confidence as the song progresses. She's really having a good time. And then, the music suddenly cuts out and AVA's left singing the song on her own. For a moment, she doesn't realise the music's abandoned her. When she does, she croaks on in a panic.

AVA (*singing, not terribly well*). She'll tease you . . . she'll appease you . . . she'll expose you . . . she's got . . . Bette Davis eyes.

And on and on she sings, in a haphazard, tuneless manner. TINA cocks her head, as if she hears AVA singing.

TINA. I recognise that voice.

CALVIN. What voice?

AVA (*completely breaking down*). Oh fuck damn damn DAMN. Why does NOTHING ever turn out right for me?

AVA smashes the guitar to the floor repeatedly.

AVA. Okay okay – you want a show? I'll give you a show. This is my Pete Townsend imitation. See. It's good, right? SEE. SEE.

CALVIN. My brother's in trouble. (*Beat.*) Why do I say that?

TINA. I *know* that voice.

AVA. All right, you happy you motherfuckers? This is my generation. MY GENERATION. MY GENERATION.

Lights up on SUZY and LESTER at Greene and Greene pawn shop, Earls Court. LESTER wears an ill fitting suit. His hair is slicked back and generally, he's made an attempt to look business like and oddly stylish. SUZY wears a sandwich board sign with the words KATE BUCK *written all over it. She speaks through a megaphone.*

SUZY. Something's coming don't know when don't know why something's coming don't know how don't know where watch your back watch your toasters your guitars your electric blankets something's coming.

LESTER. Would you shut that door and come back on in here, woman? Hell. Pawn shop's an awful sad place to conduct business without some screaming harpy discouraging customers.

SUZY (*speaks to* LESTER *through the megaphone*). Why is it sad?

LESTER. We got other people's sad old stuff all over the place. It's like limbo.

TINA. That voice is a voice that's close to me.

Lights up on the interior of a jumbo jet. TOM, LORETTA *and* BABY RAY *are passengers. So are* MARTIN *and* OTTO. MARTIN *is even sicker. He still wears only his briefs and peaked cap.*

LORETTA. I can't believe the only flight we could get was a flight to Vegas.

TOM. I don't mind. I like deserts.

LORETTA. Maybe I can get one of them quickie divorces in Vegas.

MARTIN. Senator Higgins Congressman Higgins Governor Higgins President Martin . . . Martin . . . Martin . . . HIGGINS.

OTTO. Aren't you putting the cart before the horse?

CALVIN hits a jackpot. It's a big one. Lights, bells, sirens.

CALVIN. Ohmygod I've won. To hell with history. I'VE WON.

TINA. I can't place the voice, though. Why can't I place something so near to me?

AVA (*ripping the stings from the guitar*). My generation my generation my generation MY GENERATION.

KATE *enters the pawn shop. She clocks* SUZY*'s sandwich board sign.* SUZY *clocks* KATE. SUZY *drops her megaphone.*

LESTER. You maybe wanna buy a ring, miss? We got 'em real cheap.

SUZY (*to* KATE). It's you. It's really you. It's you. It's always been you.

SUZY *moves towards* KATE. CALVIN*'s jackpot grows and grows. He's delighted.* TINA *strains to identify a voice she can't place.* AVA*'s sunk to the ground, the broken pieces of her guitar gathered in her arms. She rocks back and forth, back and forth – a steady rhythm. The lights begin a slow and persistent dimming.*

SUZY. The eclipse. It's here.

KATE. Not yet. Please. Not yet.

LORETTA. Oooo Tom, look at the sun. Look at it growing bigger in the sky.

TOM. Are we in Egypt? I see a pyramid.

LORETTA. Baby Ray, looky: the sun's getting bigger and darker and ain't it just *something* to witness?

MARTIN. Almost home Senator Higgins almost home Congressman Higgins almost home home there there home there home there.

OTTO. Spectacular. Sunset over the land that time forgot.

The lights dim ever more quickly, the casino sounds intensify, the very sky seems to close in on itself. Quick blackout. Music in: 'Go West' (Pet Shop Boys version). Lights up suddenly on TINA *and* BABY RAY, *alone in the landscape.* BABY RAY *is on the ground.* TINA *picks him up.*

TINA. Sweet baby. Awww. Sweetie pie. Where'd you come from, honey? You drop out of the sky or something? I had a baby once. Yes indeedy, sugar lips, I had one and I lost one and now I found one again. You like salad, pretty baby?

And two by two, the others, except for OTTO, *wander in from every conceivable entrance, shaken and dazed and unsure of where they are. The pairs should be:* AVA *and* SUZY; TOM *and* LESTER; LORETTA *and* CALVIN; KATE *and* MARTIN. SUZY *holds a toaster.*

AVA (*clocks* TINA). Ma? Ma?

TINA (*to* BABY RAY). I got a trailer and a portable t.v. and my oh my I know that voice, pretty baby. I know it. Coo coo coo coo, little sunshine.

LORETTA. Lester. Is that you, Lester?

LESTER. Loretta. It's me. It's . . . impossible. Where are we, Loretta?

TOM. Is this Roanoke?

KATE. Ava. Where've we got to?

AVA. Ma. Ma. MA?

TOM. Suzy. We went someplace, didn't we?

SUZY. We went back. Or forwards. I'm not sure. (*Beat; she holds out the toaster to* TOM.) In any event, I brought a gift.

TOM *takes the toaster.*

CALVIN. Martin. Martin, I'm here.

MARTIN (*he's the sickest he's ever been*). You're there. I feel good, Calvin. Strong. Some bastard made me sick, so sick. But now I'm fine and full of purpose.

CALVIN. Whenever I see you I have the urge to cry. But I don't.

MARTIN. What time is it, Calvin? Every time I see you, you look the same.

CALVIN. And you look different. That's probably why I feel I should cry.

MARTIN. Where's my time? Where is it?

MARTIN *and* CALVIN *move towards each other tentatively. A beat, before they embrace as if they're holding on for dear life. And then, a sudden unearthly rumbling sound from the deepest bowels of the earth. The sphinx/pyramid splits open to reveal* OTTO, *like Samson, pushing its walls apart.*

OTTO. What's your desire what's the situation I'll tell you the situation: I've got booze I've got car stereos I've got fax modems I've got what you want I've got what you want I've got what you WANT.

OTTO laughs, a deep, malevolent, continuous laugh. The very walls seem to shake. And then: Music out, as BABY RAY *begins to cry, a wail, a pent-up burst of frustrated emotion. Everybody turns to look at* BABY RAY.

TINA (*to* BABY RAY). Oh little boy, you can't cry. Dontcha know you're in *Vegas*? You're gonna love it here. There's lots of action. And chance. So much chance it gives you goose bumps. How about I call you Marshall? Would you like that, baby? You know what we got, Marshall? We got possibilities, little fella, endless possibilities.

And then there is stillness, as they all listen to BABY RAY's *oddly unsettling cry.*

Blackout. End of play.

A Nick Hern Book

The Strip first published in Great Britain in 1995
by Nick Hern Books Limited, 14 Larden Road, London W3 7ST
in association with the Royal Court Theatre, Sloane Square,
London SW1W 8AS

Front cover photo by Alison Hepburn, reproduced with permission

Lines on page 8 reproduced from *Who Were the Romans* by permission of Usborne Publishing © 1993 Usborne Publishing Ltd

Typeset by Country Setting. Woodchurch, Kent TN26 3TB
Printed by Cox and Wyman Ltd, Reading, Berks

A CIP catalogue record for this book is available from
the British Library

ISBS 1-85459-223-8